Ann-Marie,

Eucharist is Jesus'
all-powerful love and life
becoming enfleshed in us,
making us sources of hope
and salvation for others.

Fr. Paul

Xmas '81

Bread broken and shared

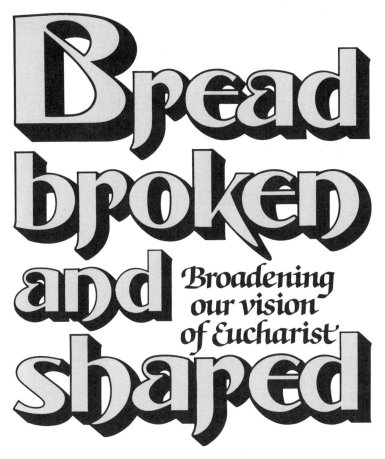

Bread broken and shared

Broadening our vision of Eucharist

PAUL BERNIER, sss

AVE MARIA PRESS   Notre Dame, Indiana

Paul Bernier, a member of the Blessed Sacrament fathers, is the editor of *Emmanuel* Magazine. A native of Pawtucket, Rhode Island, he studied for the priesthood in Blessed Sacrament seminaries, earned a master's degree from John Carroll University and has studied at Loyola (Chicago) and Creighton University. He is also the author of *Bread from Heaven* (Paulist Press, 1977).

Grateful acknowledgment is made to the following publishers: Darton, Longman & Todd Ltd., and Doubleday & Company Inc., N.Y., for excerpts from *The Jerusalem Bible,* copyright © 1966 by Darton, Longman & Todd Ltd., and Doubleday & Company Inc.

Imprimi Potest: Donald Pelotte, SSS
                Provincial Superior, Province of St. Anne
                June 5, 1981

International Standard Book Number: 0-87793-231-X (Cloth)
                                     0-87793-232-8 (Paper)
Library of Congress Catalog Card Number: 81-67539

Printed and bound in the United States of America.

Cover and text design: Carol A. Robak

CONTENTS

I

BROTHERS AND SISTERS OF JESUS

When a baby is baptized in the Eastern church, it receives not only a total immersion in the waters of life, but it is given a few drops of the precious blood as well. The day of baptism is also the day of first Communion. While it is easy enough for us in the West to understand the symbolism and beauty of using immersion, rather than the pouring of only a few drops of water on the forehead, we are not as prepared to see how a young baby can or should receive Communion.

The Eastern church, however, has never varied in linking the sacraments of initiation together both in theory and in practice. Baptism, Confirmation, Eucharist were always understood as the entry into Christian life. Hence, they were inseparable. It might be profitable, then, to begin a discussion of the Eucharist with a few basic thoughts on the true nature of Christian baptism. In fact, unless baptism is properly understood, the Eucharist cannot be fully appreciated.

Why baptism?

Of all the answers given to this question, the most common one is that baptism is necessary for salvation. It achieves this by removing original sin and its effects in our lives. The process also makes its recipients adopted children of God, thereby entitling them to enter heaven as part of their inheritance. As the first of the sacraments, it is a necessary prelude to our ability to receive the Eucharist in Communion. It has always been regarded as fundamental.

Indeed, most of us have thrilled to the stories of the great saints who literally gave their lives to spread the message of Jesus. St. Francis Xavier, for example, baptized thousands of people. The Jesuits did likewise here in North America, risking a particularly horrible martyrdom at the hands of the Iroquois in order to do so. And, to be sure, most Catholic parents seek baptism for their children as soon as possible, in order to assure them a place in the kingdom of Jesus.

A problem may lurk here. We can come to see baptism essentially as an automatic pass necessary to get us into heaven (providing we don't do anything sinful enough to lose it). Focusing on the benefits received, however, is a rather passive pastime. It's all privilege and no personal production. Is this the language and thinking of the early church?

Not really.

St. Mark's Gospel, for example, the first to be written, seldom mentions baptism explicitly. But it presupposes it throughout. In fact, we can read the Gospel as a prolonged catechesis of baptism's purpose and effects. St. Mark gives us the story of Jesus, surely, but he does so in order that we who share his life through baptism might better know what it means to become a follower of Jesus.

A quick literary analysis of the Gospel shows that it is structured to answer two basic questions: Who is Jesus? Who is the disciple? We have a partial answer in the eighth chapter, when we finally arrive at Peter's (and our?) confession of Jesus' true identity: He is the messiah. But this realization came only after struggling from misunderstanding to misunderstanding. Even the ability to state that Jesus is the messiah, however, is to win only half the battle. It is equally necessary to know what *kind* of messiah Jesus really was.

The surprising thing about all this is that Jesus seems misunderstood by the very ones who should appreciate him most: the Pharisees, those people so faithful to the Law; his own family and hometown; even his own disciples. The only ones who seem to know who he is are the pagans whose lives he touched, like the man from Gerasa who was freed from a legion of spirits and begged to become a disciple, and the Syro-Phoenician woman who trusted him implicitly and had her daughter healed as a result.

One of the basic reasons for this incomprehension is that it is impossible to say who Jesus is without at the same time affirming who the Christian is. It is impossible to divorce a true Christology from the consequences that affect our own life and action. Even to say, with Peter, that Jesus is the messiah leaves unanswered the very real ways in which we must refine our understanding of what it means to be a messiah, and how Jesus himself was to live that role. It is his example that is the standard for us.

11

Hence, the second half of the Gospel tries to purify the disciples' understanding. Jesus began to spell out what kind of messiah he was sent to be, and what this implied for his followers. His was not to be the path of war and earthly glory. He was not going to lead victorious armies against the Romans and set up an earthly kingdom which he would rule. Rather, he would undergo great sufferings and rejection and would be put to death. This was hardly popular messianic expectation.

Jesus never seems to have succeeded too well in getting his followers to understand this. In fact, each time he predicted the inevitability of his suffering and death he was misunderstood by his closest followers. Mark gives us three such incidents. Even at the Last Supper, though Peter and the disciples swear to their willingness to die for Jesus, if necessary, we are told that, in the garden only hours later, "the disciples all deserted him and ran away." It was the culmination of years of lack of understanding.

St. Mark is doing more than chronicling sad incidents in the life of Jesus. Rather, he wants us to understand that the lack of comprehension of what it means to follow Jesus is a recurrent problem in the Christian community. It is still easier for us today to focus on the personal benefits of baptism while ignoring the responsibilities which this same baptism implies. Notice what happens if we put ourselves in the place of the disciples when Jesus predicts his passion and look on their reaction as an extended teaching on the nature of baptism.

When Peter first reacts to Jesus' saying that he had to undergo great sufferings by taking him by the arm and disagreeing vehemently with him (Mk 8:32), Jesus is equally vehement with Peter. Concerned especially that Peter's example would sway the others, Jesus looked at his disciples while rebuking Peter. "The way you think is not God's way but man's," Jesus told him. You are tempting the others to think likewise—the role of Satan. "Follow *me*, Peter, not the wisdom of the world." That, incidentally, is how the "get thee behind me" phrase should be understood. For Mark uses exactly the same words in the next sentence, when Jesus calls all the people to himself as well as the disciples and issues an invitation and a general principle: "If anyone wants to be a follower of mine, let him renounce himself, and take up his cross and follow me" (8:34). We are all invited to "get behind Jesus" and to follow him not just part way, but all the way, even to death itself. Baptism is an invitation to follow Christ the whole way, to live and die as he did.

The second prediction is equally clear on this point (9:31-37). Not only did the disciples not understand what Jesus was saying, Mark tells us that they were even afraid to ask. Their behavior, however, showed that they had missed the point completely. No sooner had Jesus mentioned that he must suffer, than they put the thought out of their minds and spent the rest of the journey discussing which among them was the greatest. Jesus' patience with them was astounding. He sat down and called the Twelve to him and explained again that if any one of them wanted to be first, it would have to be by becoming last, by serving all the others.

This was the path that Jesus himself had chosen. His greatness came not from his ability to lord it over others, but from having become the servant of all. The disciple could not hope for any different path to greatness or to success. The way of those who follow Christ must be the path he himself has demonstrated. Baptism is a reality which engages us to follow Jesus and to be great in the same way that he was great: by excelling in service of others.

The final prediction of the passion shows most clearly Mark's intent. Once again, Jesus describes in graphic detail what was about to happen to him (10:33-45). And, just as predictably, the minds of the disciples are elsewhere, on thoughts of glory and prestige. In fact, John and James beat the others to Jesus to ask for the two best jobs in the new kingdom which they still expected Jesus to inaugurate. It is at this point that Jesus came right out and told them that they did not know what they were talking about. "Can you drink the cup that I must drink," he asked, "or be baptized with the baptism with which I must be baptized?" We have here a clear linking of baptism with suffering and death.

The irony of this section of the Gospel is that the other disciples were indignant at John and James. But not because they were eager to correct their deplorable lack of sensitivity. They wanted the top positions for themselves! Once again, however, Jesus reinforced the lesson. Whoever wants to be great must serve all, and whoever would be first must be the willing slave of all. Why? Because Jesus himself has given the example and pointed the way. "For the Son of Man himself did not come to be served but to serve, and to give his life as a ransom for many" (10:45).

Thus far we are familiar with the point Mark is

stressing: Those who engage themselves to follow Christ must do so all the way, must be prepared to embark on the same path that Jesus did and not shrink at the thought of suffering. This seems obvious enough. However, perhaps we have never realized all the implications of this theology. To see it only as an exhortation to offer up the pains and sufferings of life after the example of Jesus is insufficient. To go further and say that we should accept the full consequences of the human condition as did Jesus, though important, is still too weak.

Linking baptism and the passion of Jesus forces us to ask once more why Jesus suffered and died. Christian theology has always answered that in only one way: It was not for his own sins that Jesus died—for he was sinless; rather, he died for our sins. Jesus lived and died not for himself but for others. It is precisely this "for-otherness" which constitutes his greatness. Now, if baptism joins us to this aspect of Jesus' life, then what we are being told is that for those who have been baptized in Christ, life can only consist in living— and dying—for others. Baptism is a commitment to join in Jesus' redemptive style of life and to offer our own lives for the salvation of the world.

This doctrine of Jesus as the model of the baptized Christian runs through the Scriptures. At baptisms we often hear the text of Paul to the Romans (6:3-4): "You have been taught that when we were baptized in Christ Jesus we were baptized in his death; in other words, when we were baptized we went into the tomb with him and joined him in death, so that as Christ was raised from the dead by the Father's glory, we too might live a new life." That new path is uniting ourselves so fully with Christ's own life-purpose, that we no longer live for ourselves but for others. In that way we can "make up all that still has to be undergone by Christ for the sake of his body, the church" (Col 1:24). If we return to St. Mark, we can see him hurling a challenge at each of us: When we are asked to actually live the fullness of the Christ-life, will we decide that the price is too high and abandon our commitment? Or will we proclaim the good news of Christ's victory over death itself, a triumph made possible only by not fearing or avoiding the ultimate test?

When the final scene of Jesus' life begins, his followers are with him in the garden. Supposedly, they have been fully trained, and are committed to him; they are ready for the final trial. Yet, when Judas and the crowd come to seize Jesus, the disciples all desert him and run away. There is in the garden, however, a mysterious young man—and the Greek word indicates that he is a youth barely emerged from childhood, one just taking upon himself adult responsibilities. He is there, furthermore, wearing only a shroud; he is wearing the same garment that Jesus was buried in. We might well ask what a person taking his first adult steps was doing at night in the garden wearing nothing but a shroud. Why would Mark, usually so terse, introduce this seemingly extraneous bit of information in the most solemn part of the Gospel?

Mark speaks of this nameless person because he is important to his theology of baptism. He is surely the type of so many other unnamed Christians who have taken upon themselves the responsibilities of baptism. He is there as a newly baptized, still wearing his baptismal robe (symbolic of his being buried with Christ in likeness to his death), and, having committed himself to following Jesus, he is there with him in the garden. He saw Jesus seized; but when they came to seize him as well, when he came face to face with the full demands that baptism made of him of suffering and dying like Jesus, he lost his courage, abandoned his baptismal commitments, and fled. He left the robe, the sign of his willingness to offer his life with Jesus for the salvation of the world, and ran away stripped of the only garment which identified him and gave purpose to his life.

We are somewhere in that story. The choice offered that newly baptized youth eventually faces us all. Whether we react as he did will depend in large measure on whether or not we have accepted our full responsibility and learned to "take up our cross daily" and follow Jesus. Following Christ to the cross, however, will never be possible if we see baptism essentially as a personal prerogative, a freeing from (original) sin, a rite whose primary purpose is to make us heirs of heaven.

We will inherit heaven the same way that Jesus did, as the reward of a life lived totally for others. Resurrection was the crown of his sufferings and death. This gift of himself for the life of the world is what we commemorate in the Eucharist. Baptism is the initiation into this mystery. Living it fully implies that we shift the primary focus from self to others. If life has no purpose beyond "saving our souls" we will never have the courage to follow Jesus all the way to the cross. We will be like the young man in the garden—willing to follow as long as not too much is asked, yet unable to make the total sacrifice of self.

How can we insure that we do not relive his mistake? Fortunately for us, the young man can speak for himself in that regard. For he returns at the end of Mark's Gospel. He is sitting there in the tomb, clothed again, able to tell the women who came on Easter Sunday that Jesus had truly risen. This is the daily task of every true disciple—to spread the message that Christ is truly risen—a message, incidentally, that must go beyond words. It is not in *telling* people that Christ has risen that we will flood them with conviction. It is living a life that is made possible only by our belief in Christ's resurrection that will make the difference. For that conviction is what makes suffering acceptable, the knowledge that it is redemptive, that it is not futile. We tell the world that Jesus has risen when our own lives have been transformed by the power of his resurrection and we, like him, can joyfully live and die for the salvation of the world.

The Eucharist is a sacrament which perpetuates this aspect of Jesus' life and gives us the strength to pattern our lives after his. It nourishes the life begun in baptism. No wonder the Eastern church gives Communion with baptisms!

II

FINDING THE EUCHARIST IN
THE NEW TESTAMENT

At first glance, the title of this chapter might seem to promise little of interest. After all, what's difficult about finding the Eucharist in the New Testament? All we have to do is turn to the accounts of the Last Supper, where we learn all about the first Mass.

Yet, a strange thing happens when we go there. The first thing that strikes us is that the four accounts we now have differ in their telling of the story. We notice, secondly, that St. John could spend three chapters on the Last Supper and never mention the institution of the Eucharist as we imagine it. Our attempts at historical criticism in order to discover exactly what Jesus said and did on that last evening of his life seem strangely doomed to failure.

We are then struck with a further realization: The four accounts of the Eucharist that we now possess were not written primarily to teach us about the

Eucharist! Rather, in each case, the writers used an accepted liturgical tradition—one familiar to their readers—as a means to develop a further truth.

St. Paul, for example, was the first to appeal to the liturgy in this fashion. The 11th chapter of his first letter to the Corinthians, written around the year 57, shows that Paul was considerably displeased with their behavior. In those days, at least in the Antiochian churches, Eucharist was still celebrated as part of a full meal. Sundays provided the occasions when the Christians would gather and share a meal in conscious continuity with the Jesus who had lived among them. They came together in his name and recalled the mandate he had given them on the night before he died to "do this in memory of me." Hence it was only natural for them to strive to imitate his concern for others and the totality of his gift of self at that time. It was during these weekly gatherings that the needs of the community would be taken care of. Even food would be shared in common, with the brethren bringing enough so that the poorer members of the community would have plenty. It was a real Christian potluck supper.

In theory it should have worked, and it did for a decade or so. But when Paul wrote to the Corinthians, things were already starting to break down. Factions were beginning to develop, and cliques were forming even as they gathered to celebrate the Lord's Supper. The rich were bringing good food and drink for themselves and their friends, and leaving the poor to fend for themselves. It was hardly the model of community concern that Jesus had demonstrated.

How did Paul correct them? By appealing to the Eucharist itself (1 Cor 11:23-27). He reminded them of what they had been taught and showed how their behavior was a complete contradiction of what they were supposedly celebrating. So much so that it was no longer the Lord's Supper that they were celebrating but their own selfishness and self-centeredness. Paul speaks of Eucharist as a reality which all knew and could agree on, in order to make a statement about the quality of the Christian life of the Corinthians. The main thing Paul was concerned with was what it means to live as brothers and sisters of Jesus.

If we turn to the three other eucharistic narratives, found in the synoptic Gospels (Mt 26:26-29; Mk 14:22-35, Lk 22:17-20), we sense immediately that their concerns are quite different from Paul's. They also appealed to the liturgy, and quoted the liturgical texts with which all were familiar. This time it was not so much Christian behavior which they were trying to bring in line. Rather, situating these texts in the heart of Jesus' last days, their concern was to use the Eucharist to clarify the meaning of Jesus' suffering and death.

Today we hardly think twice about the shock caused by Jesus' passion. We hang crucifixes in our homes and churches as if it were only natural for the Son of God to die. Yet the crucifixion of Jesus was a tremendous blow to his followers. Not only did the hopes of the disciples come crashing down, but an agonizing effort was needed to understand the plan of God. It was even more difficult trying to explain this plan to those with whom one wanted to share the good news. Whether the audience might be Jewish or Roman or Greek, presenting a victim of state execution as messiah, or Son of God, was a difficult task indeed.

The Eucharist, however, was a marvelously suitable vehicle for doing this. Eucharist, with its multiplicity of biblical themes, shed light not only on the meaning of Christ's life, but on his death as well. By seeing his suffering and death in the light of God's past actions, one could make sense of it all. Thus, the blood of the new covenant not only betokened God's initiative and special protection, but brought to mind Jeremiah's prediction of a covenant (31:31-34) in which sin would be forgiven. And the sacrificial theme of Passover, with its lamb whose blood was the salvation of the Hebrews, also recalled the Isaian vision of the suffering servant who would voluntarily offer his life for the salvation of others (Is 42:1-9, 49:1-6, 50:4-11, 52:13-53:12). This also gave meaning and purpose to Christ's death. Again, recalling the Lord's Supper was an apt vehicle for enlightening understanding of the whole of Jesus' life and death.

If, then, we can't find primary teaching about the Eucharist in the Last Supper narratives, where else should we go? Two remarks are in order before we attempt an answer.

First of all, there is really no such thing as a New Testament theology of Eucharist. There are several theologies of Eucharist. Because we are familiar with the entire New Testament, and have convenient copies we can carry around with us, we have, over the years, arrived at a marvelous synthesis of what is found scattered throughout the New Testament. We use one Gospel to fill out another, and draw on the teaching of the epistles in the same way. But the early church was not graced with this vision. Nor was life and practice the same, for example, in Jerusalem, in Antioch, or in the Johannine communities. These were independent centers of growth and understanding. Hence, what we find from place to place are partial glimpses of a particular community's understanding. We are the ones who try to put all this together into some manageable whole.

The second remark is somewhat related. Today we speak blithely of the *Eucharist,* a term that is found nowhere in the New Testament. (It comes from the *Didache,* at the end of the first century.) Yet, there is a wealth of theology imbedded in the term. To use the word "Eucharist" has different connotations from *Mass,* or *Blessed Sacrament,* or *liturgy.* Each term emphasizes one or another aspect of a mystery which goes beyond words. And we have almost two thousand years of practice and of reflection which further shape our understanding. At least we didn't have to invent the very language we use!

The New Testament problem was unique: to find words to describe an experience of coming together as a community to share a meal at which Christ was both participant and nourishment. In wrestling to wrap words around this reality, which gave the members of the community their entire reason for existence, they had to grope and grow in the appreciation of what we might be tempted to take for granted.

That being said, here are several suggestions for reading the New Testament from a eucharistic perspective. Note that this is not quite the same thing as saying that we are looking for passages which are directly related to the Eucharist. It rests on the assumption that, since the Eucharist is central to the reality which is the church, it would be best to proceed like Paul and the evangelists and filter the entire New Testament through a eucharistic prism.

We should probably begin with the letters of St. Paul, simply because they were the first elements of the New Testament to be written. Since the Second Vatican Council, many have noticed that the new greetings, thanksgivings, and blessings that form part of the revised rites are often taken bodily from the epistles. We rejoice that more of the Scriptures are being incorporated into the liturgy. It would seem, however, that the liturgy is where they originated in the first place. Paul used these already liturgical expressions and incorporated them into his letters, because he knew that they were going to be read during the liturgy. Thus, he tied in his message with the consecrated phrases and expressions of the praying community. The same is true of many other epistle passages as well, not only the greetings or blessings. The hymns, or the credal statements (which are also found in Acts) all had their origin in the eucharistic assembly. And Paul does a beautiful job of weaving these in to reinforce his message.

Does he want to speak about concern for others and oppose rivalry and pride? He can fall back on a beautiful hymn (Phil 2:5-11) and tell us that we should let our bearing toward one another arise out of our life in Christ, who "though he was in the form of God, did not deem equality with God something to be grasped at, but rather he emptied himself, taking the form of a slave." There are many such examples, and some translations of the New Testament (especially the Jerusalem and the New American Bibles) make this easier for us to notice by setting these passages off in metrical form, or telling us in the notes.

We see, then, Paul consciously incorporating liturgical formulas into his letters. These are a direct link to the eucharistic life of the early church. Also, we should remember that Paul wrote his letters knowing that they would be read in the community liturgies. In this sense, they all deal with situations that arose in the eucharistic assemblies, and give us added insight into what the Christian community can and should be.

This same principle can be used for the Gospels. St. John explicitly tells us that he made no attempt to chronicle everything that Jesus said and did. This leaves us with the basic question of why any of the evangelists chose what they did to flesh out the story of his life. The most obvious answer is that certain incidents and teachings were remembered because they answered a particular need within the community. It is the ability to apply the life and teachings of Jesus to the concrete circumstances and needs of the church in any given age that insures their survival. At any rate, it is not hard to imagine the early Christians coming together struggling with questions like the extent of mercy and forgiveness, the scope of the apostolate, relationship to the Gentiles, accepting known "sinners" into the community and a host of similar problems, and looking to the life of Jesus for a clue to the solution. The fact that it was especially when gathered at the table of the Lord that these questions were discussed and solved gives much of the Gospels a eucharistic dimension.

There are surely gospel passages which deal more

directly with Eucharist. These are the accounts, found in all four Gospels, of the miraculous feeding of the multitude (Mk 6:34-44, 8:1-9; Mt 14:13-21, 15:32-38; Lk 9:10-17; Jn 6:1-15). The eucharistic implications of this incident are forced on us especially because St. John uses it to call forth his most explicit teaching on the Eucharist. There it is that Jesus proclaims, despite the fact that many are unable or unwilling to accept his teaching, that unless we eat his flesh and drink his blood, we shall not have life within us (6:53). Besides this there is the obvious fact that all four evangelists tell the story of the miracle in eucharistic terms. Matthew and Mark even do so twice, in both a Jewish and Gentile version of the story. The fact is, that when the event is described, it is done in clearly liturgical terms. Those four great eucharistic actions found in all the Last Supper accounts—taking, blessing, breaking and giving—are found in every account of the wondrous feeding. Jesus *takes* the bread, *blesses* and *breaks* it, and *gives* it to the disciples to distribute. It sounds like we are in the midst of a Eucharist.

In point of fact, this particular incident in the life of Christ did furnish the early church with material for its earliest theological reflection on the Eucharist. It is as if the early Christians, in trying to understand their own experience of meals with the risen Christ, looked back into the life of the historical Jesus for other moments that would help them understand the meaning of their Eucharists. The one incident which provided not only continuity with the life of Jesus, but appreciation of what it meant to share the table of the Lord, was the miraculous feeding of the multitude. (More will be said about this later.)

Alerted by this to the importance of Jesus' meals, we begin to notice how often food enters into the gospel narratives. More than four dozen accounts of Jesus' eating or talking about food are found. There is almost more about food than about miracles. Another surprising thing about these meals of Jesus is that most of them are controversial. People object to those with whom he eats. Or they find fault with his teaching. There is a whole meal ministry of Jesus that provides us with yet other precious gospel stories that can deepen our understanding of Eucharist. A general principle might be: All meals in the New Testament reveal to us something of Jesus' own ministry and provide an important link with that final meal which Jesus celebrated with his closest friends. The New Testament writers and early Christians surely understood them in this way, and so should we.

Finding the Eucharist in the New Testament, then, is both a more complicated and more exciting process than we might at first have imagined. It is more complicated because if we focus only (or *mainly*) on John 6 and on the four accounts of institution that we have, we are ignoring a vast body of literature that can further flesh out the picture we are seeking. We have tried to indicate in this chapter how our vision might be broadened, knowing full well that our understanding will still be incomplete. The danger, however, is always to be satisfied with only partial vision; the full brightness of the truth might blind us and make us realize to what extent the Eucharist is a mystery of surpassing greatness and beauty. To limit ourselves to the Last Supper is to devote ourselves to doing every Sunday (and every day for those who wish) something which Jesus did only once in his lifetime. It must be more than that.

Discovering that *more* is what makes the search exciting. For as the Scriptures begin to open themselves to us, we begin to see new patterns and relationships. Especially if we view the Scriptures with a eucharistic eye, our faith-insights will reveal countless ways in which our history still speaks to us today about what it means to gather in Christ's name at the supper he has prepared for us.

III

JESUS IN OUR LIFE

Jesus gave Christians no new cult or method of worship. When we come right down to it, we of ourselves are incapable of giving God true worship. In fact, the novelty of Christian revelation is that God became man not in order to be worshiped by us, but to serve us instead. In Paul's sermon at Athens, he contrasts the true God with the gods worshiped by the pagans, and states that the greatness of the God he preaches is that, unlike anything imagined before, he did not dwell in manmade temples, nor did he need or want service at our hands. Rather, he is a God who gives everything to his creatures (Acts 17:22-31)!

In pagan cults, and even in the Old Testament, people did have worship and cult. The sacrifices offered were based on the idea of substitution; the animals slain were somehow representative of us. Their ritual slaughter symbolized what we ourselves deserved, and their blood was offered to God in lieu of our own in order to appease his wrath. That is not at all the picture of God we get in the New Testament. Not only has our way of relating to him changed, but God's reaching out to us is something which requires an acceptance on our part. We are invited to be caught up in a personal love relationship with God.

It may seem shocking to think that there is really nothing we can do for God, no way to appease him when we sin, no way to earn redemption by our deeds. The Letter to the Hebrews struggles to express this reality to people who were still very familiar with Jewish worship. It states, somewhat brusquely, that we ought not place the foundation of our faith in God in cleansing rites or sacrifices; we need a more mature view (6:1-3). The reality is that Jesus came as the fulfillment of Psalm 40, which realized that God did not want or need sacrifices and oblations. Rather, he seeks an open heart and mind; he looks for obedience to his will. This is what Jesus did so well and so completely that we have all been set on a new path to God. "In other words, brothers, through the blood of Jesus we have the right to enter into the sanctuary by a *new* way which he has opened for us..." (10:19-20).

The only "cult" that is true worship in the new covenant is to practice the same service which God himself gives to us in Christ. The wonder of revelation is that God has not left us on our own to find out something about him. This is the fate of the pagans. Instead he has told us about himself. He has shared the secrets of his own existence; his laws he has made known to us as well as his great love and desire to join us to himself. And, as the Letter to the Hebrews begins by reminding us, even the greatness of the Old Testament pales in comparison with that brought by Christ. "At various times in the past and in different ways, God spoke to our ancestors through the prophets; but, in our own time, the last days, he has spoken to us through his Son.... He is the radiant light of God's glory and the perfect copy of his nature" (1:1-3). Thus it is only through Christ that we can know or understand what type of service the Father really desires.

What do we see in Jesus? We know first of all that he was a layman. He did not belong to the priestly family, and he himself never offered any particular Temple sacrifices. The Letter to the Hebrews, the only one to call Jesus a priest, stresses the essential difference between his priesthood and any which had gone before. "So our Lord, of whom these things were said, belonged to a different tribe, the members of which have never done service at the altar; everyone knows he came from Judah, a tribe which Moses did not even mention when dealing with priests" (7:13-14). The Levitical or Aaronic priesthood had been annulled in Christ anyway because of its weakness and uselessness. Therefore Jesus' "priesthood" is of a different kind, eternal, and totally effective because it is the offering of a life completely given for others. This the author of Hebrews calls the priesthood of Melchizedek.

The essence of Jesus' priesthood lay in a complete and radical acceptance of his human condition; he chose, further, to live his life for others as a servant, for such was the Father's will. Jesus' self-gift to the Father for our sake culminated in his death on the cross. His "for-otherness" was also evident during his earthly ministry. We know that his life was one of compassion for the poor, the outcasts, the sinners. We are aware that his teaching revolved around openness to God, understanding the radical demands made by his law and the ability to go beyond legalism to discern and live the purpose of all law. His total involvement with people caused him to be accused of laxity; good people were not supposed to associate with sinners. Jesus, however, would not be swayed. He knew that true worship in spirit and truth meant that all temporal institutions would be replaced by himself and by those who possess his Spirit.

Thus Jesus is not only the revelation of God, he is also the supreme worshiper of the Father. He is the ultimate realization of all religion. In Jesus, not only was the Father's love for mankind revealed, but God showed us in him what it means for us to commit ourselves to the Father. In and through the religious service and fidelity of Jesus, God has revealed himself. He is the embodiment of religion itself. This is the Jesus whose life is epitomized and capsulized in the Eucharist. For there we have the totality of his self-gift to the Father and to us.

The true beauty of the Eucharist in this context, then, lies in what it teaches us about God's own way of life and his gift of love to us in Jesus. Even a cursory familiarity with the Scriptures shows us that we, not God, are the primary beneficiaries of this gift. In the final prediction of the passion which we have in St. Mark's Gospel (10:32-45), Jesus is very clear about his impending death. As usual, the disciples are thinking of other things. But when it becomes necessary to show John and James that their request for honors and for special positions in his kingdom is quite out of line with the meaning of his life, he asks them simply, "Can you drink the cup I shall drink?"—a clear allusion to the Eucharist which would enshrine his gift of self. We are all meant to drink of that cup and to offer our lives in ransom for others.

Jesus goes on to drive the lesson home. He insists that anyone who aspires to greatness must serve the rest: "Anyone who wants to rank first among you must be slave to all." Why? Because Jesus himself "did not come to be served but to serve, and to give his life as a ransom for many."

St. John insists on the same theme when Jesus gathers for his final supper with his closest friends. Much to their surprise, Jesus began to wash their feet (13:1-15). Again, Jesus was giving an object lesson for all time: "If I then, the Lord and Master, have washed your feet, you should wash each other's feet. I have given you an example so that you may copy what I have done to you." It is in loving service of one another that we prove ourselves true disciples, that we truly drink the cup that Jesus himself drank.

The Eucharist is a memorial, not only of Jesus' redemptive sufferings and death, but of his entire life of obedience and self-emptying. From the beginning of his public life he made a conscious choice of the role of a servant. Rather than his own will, he accepted the cup the Father had given him to drink. The Eucharist summarizes all the decisions and actions which made up Jesus' public life. His life was of whole cloth. When God chose to come among us as man, he chose not the path of glory, nor the intoxicating headiness of being a victorious messiah-king. Rather, he chose the fully human way of a defenseless human person whose life is motivated by love of others.

St. John summarizes this for us rather succinctly: "God's love for us was revealed when God sent into the world his only Son so we could have life through him; this is the love I mean: not our love for God, but God's love for us when he sent his Son to be the sacrifice that takes our sins away" (1 Jn 4: 9-10).

Sublime as is this vision of God, it is also somewhat disconcerting. It is almost too good to be true. Worse yet, most people would rather not have a God whose love—like the rain—falls on both the just and the unjust alike. Yet, we have done nothing to deserve God's love. "But what proves that God loves us is that Christ died for us while we were still sinners" (Rom 5:8). This means, however, that we have no handle on God. We can't control him by our actions. We can't merit his love; it is a gift.

When *we* give, it is usually with strings attached. We want and expect recognition. If people don't send us Christmas cards in return, we soon cross them off our list. If gifts are not reciprocated, they shortly cease. We can control our relationships in this way. But God comes into our lives uninvited. He offers to wash our feet not because we deserve it but because we need it. He is the persistent lover, who can never be repaid. We can never get even with him.

Another reason why this perspective is disconcerting is that it takes religion out of the sanctuary and church and into the marketplace. We would much rather restrict religion to the church; otherwise it might become inconvenient. It is easier if religion is a Sunday kind of thing, or if it occupies only a corner of our lives. To see Eucharist as a summary capsulization of Jesus' whole public life, to accept it as the re-presentation of a truly godly earthly life, is to recognize that it must take over and influence our entire lives. Unless our life choices, our value systems, our actions, are all informed by a eucharistic consciousness, they are not fully Christian. For the Eucharist is not just some ritual action that we offer to God; it is the life of Christ which God offers to us.

The implications of this are enormous. First of all, it tells us something about God. We come to see him as one who is loving and kind. Never need we fear him. We see him as one who is more concerned about our happiness and salvation than we are ourselves. We come to understand that God became man not to claim our homage, submission and service, but to give and spend himself for us. It is a complete reversal of our expectations and priorities.

A second consequence is that worship is not something that we give *to* God as much as it is something we get *from* him. The gifts of bread and wine that we offer at the Eucharist are transformed into the life-giving presence of Jesus and offered back to us as God's ultimate gift. We are the ones who benefit.

As the Eucharist is celebrated today, the gift comes in two packages. The first is wrapped in the Liturgy of the Word. Here is where we can immerse ourselves in those classic insights into our salvation history. We come to see God's goodness revealed especially in the life of his Son, and can measure our own lives against the compassion and generosity shown by Jesus. Thus the eucharistic gift which is presented in the second part of the liturgy takes on ever-new modalities and richness as our understanding of who Jesus is grows and matures. We are the ones who are meant to be changed by the liturgy. Our worship is simply the acceptance of God's gifts.

A third consequence is that our Eucharist, the Mass, becomes the summary of all of Christian life. We are part of the action. When we meet Christ at his table and say "Amen" to his body which is offered for us, we say, in the words of St. Augustine, amen to what we are. We meet Jesus at that table with the full reality of our persons. The effort to prove worthy of Christ's gift of himself will transform us only if we have been so personally touched by his love that we are moved to love him and give ourselves in return. Living a Christian life is not following a set of external rules. It is more than measuring up to some predetermined standard of perfection. It is a totally free and spontaneous love response which leads us to pattern our lives on the One who has given himself so willingly to us. It moves us to become Christ for others.

Yet a fourth consequence is that liturgical prayer teaches us how we should always pray. Prayer is not something we give to God so as to please him sufficiently that he will grant us what we desire. It is paganistic to pray in order to change God's mind, as though he didn't love us enough to give us what we need until we prevailed on him with our ritual, our words or our persistence. Christians pray knowing that God has already given us everything he could in his Son. Prayer then becomes an exercise in changing ourselves, not God. We come to know his will better, to see what is for our good, and to become more like the self-giving Christ.

The Eucharist is the perfect model of this kind of prayer. For not only does it present us in the Liturgy of the Word with God's own revelation of himself, but the entire Eucharistic Prayer is one long hymn of thanksgiving and praise to God for his loving goodness to us in Christ. It situates us in the proper perspective of those whose lives have been graced with every good gift the Father's love could provide. This spirit of thanks and praise should become the dominant characteristic of our prayer, for it is the root and foundation which allows us to offer our own lives as a ransom for many and to plead with our blood for the salvation of humankind. In this way we avoid getting lost in purely private prayer, because of our immersion in and consciousness of all our brothers and sisters for whom Jesus lived and died, and for whom we also strive to live.

A final consequence is that by opening ourselves to God in the Eucharist, we give him the kind of service he really wants. For he desires the world to be saved, he wants to embrace all with his love. By joining in the Eucharist of his Son, we commit ourselves to do our part to continue his mission on earth. It is by accepting our role and vocation in life as Jesus himself did, by living lives of service of others, that we begin to appreciate what the Eucharist is all about. We then please God by giving to others the same kind of service he himself first gave to us and continues to give each time we gather at the table of the Lord.

IV

UNIFYING OUR VISION

The synoptic Gospels all speak of an incident in the life of Jesus when he was asked to determine the greatest commandment in the Law. On the face of it the question was deceptively simple. But when we realize that by Jesus' time the rabbis had pinpointed some 613 commandments to be observed in the Old Testament, finding a hierarchy in all of this was quite a task. It was even more difficult for the common people, for most had no scrolls of their own, and literacy was far from universal.

Jesus was equal to the task, however. He chose two commandments as belonging together. The first one was an obvious choice; it summarized the commandments given Moses (Mt 22:34-40; Mk 12:28-31; Lk 10:25-28). "You shall love the Lord your God with all your heart, with all your soul, with all your strength, with all your mind." This was straight from Deuteronomy (6:5) and came as no surprise. What *was*

surprising was Jesus' adding to it another commandment buried in the book of Leviticus (19:18), "You shall
love your neighbor as yourself." In one fell swoop,
Jesus had unified the teaching of the whole Old Testament.

Perhaps we can use some of that same vision in
our own lives. Since the Vatican Council, so much has
changed so fast that we are sorely in need of a stable
unifying principle. Most of the liturgical laws have
been changed. We're not quite sure which of the rules
in the code of canon law still apply. We're not even certain what to mention in confession anymore; so many
things no longer seem to be sins! Many people seem
uncertain about basic church teaching also. The neat
system we once had no longer suffices. One begins to
envy the Jews having only 613 commandments to
worry about.

There is no need, however, to so complicate Christian life. The things we believe, the actions we should
perform, the way we ought to pray, the moral values
that should characterize us are not arbitrary or independent of one another. They all come together in
the person of Jesus, and that person is living still and
guiding his church. The Eucharist is our extension of
the Incarnation, and it gives us a focal point toward
which everything can and should relate.

One of the benefits of the biblical renewal in the
church since the Council has been the way it has
enriched our understanding of the Eucharist. For 400
years all eucharistic teaching was based completely
on the Council of Trent. But that teaching was
necessarily directed at defending those aspects of
Catholic doctrine that were being denied by the Prot-

estants, namely that the Mass was truly a sacrifice and that Jesus was really present in the Eucharist. Transubstantiation was also defended as the best way (so far) of explaining the reality of Christ's eucharistic presence. By 1960 though, we had become static. There had been little growth since Trent and, indeed, no real desire to extend eucharistic theology beyond what that Council had done. Today so many aspects of the eucharistic mystery can be better understood when we become aware of all the biblical themes and traditions which converge there. Some of the more obvious Old Testament themes are that of the Paschal Lamb, with its rich presentation of sacrificial self-giving; there is the biblical notion of memorial, reminding us that when we "do this in memory" of Jesus we actually insert ourselves into God's continuing saving actions in our own lives; we have also the idea of covenant.

Covenant is such an all-embracing concept that it can provide us with a good example of how Christian life can be unified and simplified if we see everything in covenant perspective. We are reminded of the reality of covenant each time the priest, in the Eucharistic Prayer, takes the cup of wine and says, "This is the cup of my blood, the blood of the new and everlasting covenant." What, then, is covenant all about?

The idea of covenant is, first of all, a basic and recurring theme in the Old Testament. It is the foundation of Israel's relationship with God as well as the motive urged on it for observance of the Torah. It is the ultimate motive for all of God's behavior toward his people. Though we can distinguish many covenants in the Old Testament, the Mosaic covenant was the last and most important. When the books of the Old Testament were written in their final form, this covenant was often presumed even years before it took place.

The idea of covenant was not an exclusively religious one. Kings made covenants with those they conquered, and people made them with each other. As the concept was taken into the religious sphere, the most obvious model was the suzerainty treaties of political history. These covenants, or alliances, were really quite simple. A superior offered to make an alliance or pact with someone; conditions were laid down; when accepted, certain relationships between the parties were established; their binding nature was usually symbolized by blood and a sign was often given to remind the participants of their agreement.

In the Mosaic covenant we can see all of these elements. First of all, the initiative was clearly on the part of God. He is the one who chose Moses to lead the people out of Egypt and who guided their wanderings in the desert. Shortly after their escape from slavery, the Lord called Moses to himself and made the tribes an offer they literally couldn't refuse. The people were told that if they obeyed the commandments which God would give them, they would become his own special people among all the nations. He would watch over them, protect them from their enemies and give them a land of their own, one flowing with milk and honey. Recognizing a good thing when they heard it, the people agreed and said that they would abide by whatever God asked of them. Moses then gave them the commandments, and, taking the blood of bulls and goats, poured half of it on the altar and sprinkled the rest on the people, symbolizing the common life which was now theirs. The basic sign of the Mosaic covenant was the observance of the sabbath, just as circumcision was for Abraham, and the rainbow for Noah.

It is obvious in reading Exodus or Deuteronomy, that many hands and several traditions have shaped the telling of the story. All of this reinterpretation bears witness to the central part that the covenant played in the history of Israel. The prophets saw all the subsequent misery of defeats in battle, exile and the destruction of the nation as caused by the people's infidelity to the covenant. They had abandoned God, and he had left them at the mercy of their enemies. All efforts at interiorization were aimed at recapturing the living values and principles of the covenant God had made with his people. The psalms are profoundly marked by realization of a special relationship with God. The covenant deeply marked the history of the Jewish people.

Covenant morality deeply marked the life of all. One of the amazing things about the story of David and Bathsheba, for example, is that it was even mentioned in the Bible. Other Oriental kings of the time could have taken any woman in the kingdom with impunity; they all belonged to the ruler. Israel's kings, though, were under covenant. David knew that he had sinned.

Central as was this sacred relationship, one prophet, Jeremiah, foresaw its being replaced. "See, the days are coming...when I will make a new covenant with the house of Israel (and the house of Judah), but not a covenant like the one I made with their ancestors on the day I took them by the hand to bring them out of the land of Egypt" (Jer 31:31-34). The new covenant, unlike the old, "would be written upon their hearts";

God's law would be within rather than on tablets of stone.

It is this reality that the Eucharist fulfills so perfectly. The institution texts in Paul and in the synoptics all speak of the blood of the covenant, or of the covenant in Christ's blood. Once again we witness the inauguration of a new people.

Like the Mosaic covenant, this one was also a free gift of God. "God loved the world so much that he gave his only Son, so that everyone who believes in him may not be lost but may have eternal life" (Jn 3:16). We stand as the beneficiaries of his love, and once again he offers us a special relationship with himself. We are to form part of that kingdom which Jesus preached and for which he lived and died. The benefits of the kingdom are many; any page of the Gospel details them. Among the greatest are the forgiveness of sins and the gift of the Holy Spirit who will remain with us and guide us in the way of Christ.

Like the Mosaic covenant there is also a law. But, in line with Jesus' own distillation of Old Testament law, it is a deceptively simple one. "I give you a new commandment: Love one another; just as I have loved you, you also must love one another." We are told that if we have this love among us, all will recognize us as his disciples (Jn 13:34-35). Chapter 15 repeats this message even more insistently and points to the extent of Jesus' love for us: giving his very life. Greater love than this no one has.

This law must be accepted by us. That is the meaning of our "Amen" at the end of the Eucharistic Prayer and before Communion. We pledge ourselves to live the one commandment that Jesus has given us, and he, in his turn, graces us with the gift of his presence.

Furthermore, this new covenant was also sealed in blood—in the very blood of Christ poured out for us and for our offenses. On the cross, as his blood was drunk by a parched earth, he offered his life and love to the Father for our sakes.

The sign of the new covenant is the Christian community itself, but only if it is an authentic loving community. All will recognize us as Jesus' followers if we truly have love for one another; which means that unless we have his sacrificial love for each other, *no one* will recognize us as belonging to him. The love commandment is the only thing that sets us apart from anyone else.

Note the importance of this commandment. For one thing, it takes in and gives the basic motivation for everything we should do. Any other commandment is ultimately reduced to this one. Thus, it helps us cut through a legalistic attitude and the habit of asking, "Is it a sin if I do this?" Such an attitude betrays a rule-centered approach to life. We follow the rules, get by with what we can, and are especially careful about the serious prescriptions (while neglecting the others somewhat). It also avoids the mind-set of people, for example, who confess missing Mass on Sunday even though they may have been sick at the time. The fear of having broken one of the rules is a dreadful tyrant; and it has no place in the church of Christ.

Rather, if we are true to the love ethic of Jesus, all our actions can become ways of showing gratitude for what he has done for us. Since we are concerned about loving a person, it no longer is a question of just following some external rule or norm. The law is truly written in our hearts, as Jeremiah foresaw, because it has been burned there by the sight of Christ on the cross, facilitating a response of thankfulness and praise in all we say and do. Motivation, then, is built in. It is not fear; it is more than naked obedience; it surpasses wanting to be perfect. It is the only way we have of showing Jesus and the world that we are truly his followers. Nothing else will make us unique.

The Law of Christ, in its full covenant force, implies that we have thrown away all the minimums, that we no longer look to external norms for justification, but only to the grace of God. To impose an external standard on everyone may be necessary for public order, but it says nothing of merit or of grace. And it holds everyone—young or old, advanced or just beginning, crippled or healthy—to the same norm. Covenant morality asks us to realize that if we have been graced more, more will be expected of us. As our love grows, so will the demands that we will make willingly upon ourselves. Greater love than this no one has....

Note, finally, that we show our love for Christ not directly, but by how we love our fellow men and women. St. John put it simply: "Anyone who says, 'I love God,' and hates his brother, is a liar" (1 Jn 4:20). Jesus' commandment implies that our relationships with our neighbor are no longer based on expediency or self-interest ("love your neighbor as yourself"), but on what we have personally received from him ("love as I have loved you"). Hence, to say "Amen" to Christ at Mass, to accept the covenant, is to accept neighbor as part of the same relationship. The more Christ's example gentles our approach to others, the more we can say that we truly love him. Then people will say once again, "See how they love one another."

The basic truths of our faith, the central beliefs on which our salvation rests, are all found in the covenant mystery: God the Father loving us to the extent of sending his Son, who shed his blood as the mediator of a new covenant between God and his creatures. The trinitarian relationships, the role of Christ in salvation and the role of the Holy Spirit in guiding the church are all included. Whatever truths the church teaches, the creed, are all part of this mystery of our salvation, either as it pertains to God's initiative or to our response.

Also, no matter how many changes may occur in liturgical practice, in teaching emphasis, or in the explanation of Christian morality, nothing should touch or weaken our relationship with Jesus and through him with the Father. This is a covenant bond sealed in the very blood of Jesus and as solid as the cross on which he died. We no longer need make distinctions between "moral" theology (for average people) and "spiritual" theology (for the more perfect)! Rather, everything we do should be expressive of love of neighbor. This forces us to see our lives in terms of actively doing something to spread Christ's love in our world. It is not enough simply to do no wrong; we are expected to do right. Love is a positive reality.

St. Paul put it well when he told us that whether we eat or drink, or whatever we do, it should be all for the glory of God (1 Cor 10:31). In the past it was easy to live with two compartments in our lives: One was for our religious actions and prayers, the other was for all the other actions of our everyday life. We can't com-

BREAD BROKEN AND SHARED

partmentalize a covenant relationship. Whatever we do either brings us closer to Christ or further away from him. All of life is related to that "Amen" we utter to close the Eucharistic Prayer and with which we greet the Body of Christ. For we say "Amen" to the one whose blood was shed, making possible a whole new relationship with God and with each other. Whatever helps us better understand the God who has made all this possible, or the ways in which he wants us to show our sincere love for one another, is yet another blessing of the new and everlasting covenant.

V

CALLED TOGETHER IN CHRIST

In his First Letter to the Corinthians, St. Paul has a frightening statement. He refers to their eucharistic celebrations and tells them sharply that it is not really the Eucharist which they are celebrating (1 Cor 11:20). What was lacking was not something as prosaic as proper bread or wine, or the prescribed words or rubrics for a Eucharistic Prayer. It was far more serious, and went right to the heart of what our liturgy is all about: They weren't behaving as members of one community. Because their behavior contradicted their liturgical celebration, the Eucharist itself was rendered useless—null and void.

If we admit that the same thing can happen today, then we are saying that it is possible for us to be completely correct liturgically and still have meaningless and fruitless Eucharists. We can go on this way for years and never grow; in fact, we can regress because of the scandal we give or because the example of our lives bears no witness to the reality of Christ's love and grace. Instead of being a celebration of life in Christ, the Eucharist can become a sterile pageant reinforcing us in personal selfishness and sin.

We know that the Eucharist has always characterized the Christian community ever since Jesus asked us to "do this in memory" of him. Throughout the centuries, Jesus' followers have met to break bread in his name. It has endured and has been celebrated in all the corners of the world. Millions gather each week to share the Lord's Supper. The one danger which has revealed itself down through the ages is that, rather than being shaped and formed by what we celebrate, we have succeeded in domesticating the Eucharist so that it does not disturb our sinful and selfish lives. Many think it so.

We in the Western world are being accused by our Third World brethren of having so etherealized or spiritualized the Eucharist that it has been possible to colonize and dominate peoples the world over while celebrating the Eucharist over the bodies of the conquered and oppressed. Exploiters could piously meet in liturgical correctness and splendor and leave church to continue conquest. Through all this, the Eucharist itself has seldom forced us to question our assumptions. Instead of official worship calling everyone to a new freedom in Christ, it has been brought into a weak and anemic supporting role only reinforcing the status quo.

Perhaps we should begin by seeing how, even at the beginning of Christianity, Jesus' sacrificial meal could be misused. The problems in the Corinthian church are critical and informative for the church of all ages. If we understand what lay at the root of their situation, we might be able to avoid similar mistakes ourselves.

Note, first of all, that in the first few decades after Jesus' resurrection, the Eucharist was not the symbolic reality we know today. Rather, the Eucharist was celebrated as part of or in conjunction with a full meal which all would share in common. Everyone was to bring enough so that all might share. This was done in conscious continuity with Jesus' own practice during his lifetime, and especially in memory of the final meal which he celebrated with his disciples on the eve of his death. The memorial of that meal is where we commemorate the continuing fact of our salvation, for there Jesus' messianic deliverance is made present. At the Lord's Supper, everyone shared the one bread of Christ, making the participants one body, one community of love and salvation.

That was the theory. Paul's letter (1 Cor 11:17-34) makes it clear that a number of abuses had crept in, among them gluttony and drunkenness. This, however, is not what upsets Paul most. He scores especially the selfish indifference of individuals or groups to the needs and situation of the poor. This went right to the heart of what Eucharist was all about. To divide into factions meant not seeing the church as the expression of a new family called together in Christ. It manifested contempt for the communal nature of Christianity. Paul did not hesitate to say that in behaving in this manner people were not only sinning, they actually despised the church of God. Their lack of love and concern for others both struck at the root of the church and threatened the reality of the Eucharist.

While the whole incident is instructive of how we can fail so easily to live what we celebrate, let us isolate three principles which Paul uses. The most basic one is also the simplest: If the community dimension is lacking, the Lord's Supper is not realized. We might add that to the extent that the community aspect is missing, the Eucharist is unfruitful. Paul did not reprimand the cliques for shaming or abusing the poor, but for despising the church. By definition, the church was the whole body of believers united through Christ to one another. Lack of concern was especially destructive because it prevented the church from being recognized as the community which it should be. To ignore the very nature of the church is to despise the one who founded it. Eucharist celebrates the church's identity; it can never be a private reality.

The second principle on which Paul bases his reasoning is: Faith must be expressed in service to others, for only in this way can we serve God. Paul is not interested in simply getting the Corinthians to behave better. He wants them to know why certain behavior is proper or not. In recalling the nature of the Eucharist, Paul reminds them that the cup given them by Christ is the new covenant in his blood. We are immediately mindful of Jeremiah's prophecy concerning that covenant (31:31-34) where it is characterized as being written in the heart. The interior force provided by the example of Jesus' total gift of self should make us mindful of the new relations existing between God and his creation, and between men and women with each other. The abuses at Corinth prevented Christ's cup from taking its normal effect—freeing the recipients from personal selfishness and sin.

The third principle stresses once more the importance of community: He who eats and drinks without recognizing the body eats and drinks a judgment on himself. This goes beyond asking us to recognize that Christ is really present in the Eucharist; it asks us to recognize him as really present in the community. Unless we recognize and act upon the reality of Christ's presence in each of his brothers and sisters, we celebrate only our own condemnation. The reason for this is simple: If Christ's death is to be redemptive throughout history, it will be so only in its visible effects on the community of believers. Only in the measure that the community members live in loving union with one another will the power of Christ's redemptive death be proclaimed.

We are now living almost two thousand years after the Corinthians, and the only real question is whether the lesson they left us has entered into our consciousness and practice. There are two dangers, both of which attack the notion of community stressed by St. Paul. One is that societies, or cities, or parishes, can have offered the Eucharist weekly for many years without ever improving the relationships of the people therein. Do the rich and poor share the same table and somehow bridge the gap that seems to grow ever wider between classes, whether these are rooted in economic differences, nationality, or social class? St. Paul reminded us that we who eat the one bread become the one Body of Christ (1 Cor 10:17). The Eucharist will be spiritual food only if it brings about this oneness, only if it leads to greater love and communion among persons and groups. We cannot be blind to the factions that exist among us without making our Eucharists as fruitless and sacrilegious as the Corinthians.

A second danger results from turning the Eucharist into a private devotion. This is very easy for us to do today. We are so convinced that Jesus is present in the Eucharist and that we receive him in Communion, that our participation at Mass becomes the high point of our day and of our prayer. It is the time when we can commune with our Savior and glory in the realization of his presence within. Whether there are other people celebrating with us makes very little difference, really. Most of the time they are a distraction anyway, and we always try to sit where we won't have to be in the same pew with others. Others are not seen as part of our prayer.

We have come a long way from the early church. Then, there was only one Eucharist in any location, and all gathered for the common celebration. The whole community was involved. The liturgy was the bond of union between believers. The Acts of the Apostles tells us what the early liturgies were meant to be: "The faithful all lived together and owned everything in common; they sold their goods and possessions and shared out the proceeds among themselves according to what each one needed" (2:42-47). Another summary of the early days reads: "The whole group of believers was united, heart and soul; no one claimed for his own use anything that he had, as everything they owned was held in common...none of their members was ever in want" (4:32-35).

Even admitting the idyllic quality of these accounts, we must admit that the ideal was clear. Everyone was caught up in a first fervor, to be sure.

They belonged to a *movement,* a movement started by Jesus and guided by him which broke down the walls of separation between peoples. The equality of all in the new community was expressed in their common eucharistic meal. It was no easier for them than it is for us, and we know of grave deficiencies among them. But this still remained the ideal they strove to live by.

Recognizing the problem, however, is the first step to finding a solution. We should begin by asking whether or not years of eucharistic celebration have made any difference in our social awareness, in our commitment to justice, in the effort we make to build the world of love and unity which Jesus lived and died for. If we are little changed from what we were five or 10 years ago, then the Eucharist has become a cultic action that has little real influence in life: It has not succeeded in challenging awareness or rooting us more fully in the community it was meant to express.

A further question might focus on how one habitually celebrates Eucharist. Is it more an action of the whole community in which I am involved, or does it tend to be my own personal moment alone with Christ? While we all need time alone with God, that is not the main purpose of the eucharistic action. If the Eucharist represents the highest point of Jesus' own prayer to his Father, it must be admitted it was a dynamic expression of love to us all; it was a tremendous example of service of others to the extent of giving his entire self. Our own celebrations should strive to equal that commitment and love.

How then, can we live a truly eucharistic life, one characterized by the self-giving of Christ? We know that it doesn't happen automatically. We might best begin by asking what understanding we have of church. If we are wedded to the idea of the church as being essentially a perfect society having within itself, under the guidance of its hierarchically constituted leaders, all the sacramental means of grace which we need for salvation, we will find it rather difficult to understand it as a community of people striving together to bring about a more perfect realization of Christ's kingdom. The former idea relates us directly to the institution; provided we follow the rules and avail ourself of the helps provided, we can be assured of getting to heaven. But the church is not essentially a club with a set of rules; it is a pilgrim people en route together.

We get a false idea of perfection if we see the church as an institution with all the answers and all the directions we need for life. This approach allows us to say, once we have observed all the commandments and followed all the precepts, that we are good Christians. This can stifle further growth and prevent us from seeing how we have yet to grow. It is too static a view. A *community* understanding, however, impresses on us from the beginning that there are no set limits to love or to life. Since the basic bond is a personal one, life becomes a series of relationships. Our relationship with Jesus is expressed and grows as we grow in our relationships and concern for one another. We know we will never reach perfection here below since we can always increase in love, and because Jesus has never laid down a minimum with which he would be satisfied. Rather, he said that we would be recognized as his disciples only if we exhibited the same love for one another that he did for us (Jn 13:35).

Each time we celebrate Eucharist, we end the Eucharistic Prayer with the words "through him, with him, in him, in the unity of the Holy Spirit, all honor and glory are yours, almighty Father, forever and ever." We acknowledge that the only way to honor and please the Father is in, with and through Christ. If we are to develop a eucharistic mind and heart, we will recognize that Christ's way is the way of service to others. We will appreciate the fact that his greatest gift is his presence within the community, for that is where we should be able to find strength and support, loving care and concern. We are all meant to form part of that sharing Christian community which finds in the Eucharist the high point of its self-expression and the inspiration for continued growth.

After this, it's only a question of practice. Having reminded ourselves of true priorities, we can concentrate on two areas. The first is greater service and generosity, both within our own immediate community and without. Instead of examining our consciences each day on the things we have done wrong, we can look for what we have done *right*, how we have made the world a better and more Christlike place. We can strive to recognize Christ more easily in the poor and oppressed, remembering that Jesus himself identified with "the least of his brothers." Is it too much to expect some positive action each day on behalf of others?

Eucharist is the second area. We should celebrate with humility, knowing that we always fall short of the self-gift which it implies. Reminding ourselves that the failure of others to appreciate its community dimensions resulted in a severe judgment from the apostle will prevent us from likewise wasting our time and availing nothing for salvation. Their Eucharists were empty and fruitless. If we are to avoid the same condemnation, it will be because of the effort to recognize the Body of Christ in our world, and to express our faith in a life of service.

VI

EATING AT THE LORD'S TABLE

It is only in recent years that we have felt comfortable in thinking of the Eucharist as a meal. The fact that in years past some claimed it was *only* a meal, denying its sacrificial aspects, helped our distrust of course. So did our 400-year habit of referring to the Eucharist as Mass, Communion, and Real Presence. Such neat compartmentalization fragmented our understanding and gave us a rather static view of what is actually a dynamic action of Christ. This way of thinking also affected our practice. For years it was common for people to "assist" at Mass and not receive Communion. The church eventually had to rule that one should receive at least once a year! The meal dimension receded further and further into the background.

These attitudes are far from dead, either among the faithful or in official circles. There are still laws on the books that all Catholics have a serious obligation to "go to" Mass each Sunday, even though some are forbidden to receive Communion. That's a little like forcing someone to go to a banquet and allowing him only to smell the food.

At any rate, thinking of Eucharist in terms of a meal has an ancient and honorable tradition. From St. John we read, "If you do not eat the flesh of the Son of Man and drink his blood, you will not have life in you" (Jn 6:53). And again, "My flesh is real food and my blood is real drink" (6:55). Furthermore, all four evangelists see eucharistic implications in Jesus' wondrous feeding of the multitudes, and the synoptics narrate the institution of the Eucharist in the course of a Passover meal which Jesus shared with his disciples.

There is also one very good practical reason for focusing on the meal values of the Eucharist: All of us eat. Eating is an important social ritual in which we all share. Children are always hungry. I remember the first theological problem I faced as a priest came from a sixth grader who asked me to solve a class problem. Would we *eat* in heaven? I told him *no*, only to see his face fall and hear him exclaim, "Gosh, Father, eating's half the fun of living!" In understanding the mysteries of God, it is easier to go from the known to the unknown. Jesus did this so often, and he did choose a meal as the vehicle of his self-gift. By appreciating the values inherent in meals, we might better appreciate certain aspects of the Eucharist as well.

The human values expressed by meals have been lost somewhat in American society. Latin cultures have a far better understanding of the social implications surrounding meals. In the McDonald's society which is ours, we can actually make the mistake of thinking that the most important thing about mealtimes is the *food*. With all the activities of modern life, many families are seldom together for meals, and that compounds the problem. The best example we have to aid our understanding are special meals shared on festive occasions, be they holidays or times we invite others to our table.

Everyone enjoys receiving dinner invitations ... and not primarily for the food! The thoughtfulness of the one extending the invitation, the pleasure of gathering with friends, the conversation and conviviality, all play most important roles. If these are all present, even if the food is not the most sumptuous, we will look back on that occasion and say, "That was a good meal!" It is obvious that in meals of this type, the social relationships are the most important realities. Good friends make any food taste better.

If this is true for us, it was even more true in the time of Christ. In Near-Eastern society, meals were sacred. To break bread with someone was a pledge of solidarity and friendship. During more formal meals, there would be much dialogue and sharing. Jesus, in fact, carried on a rather extensive ministry of meal-fellowship. Because the scribes and Pharisees understood the real meaning of meals, they often objected to the people Jesus was eating with. The fact that Jesus was regarded as a rabbi by many, a prophet by some, and that he would associate himself with tax collectors, prostitutes, those who did not know (and hence could not keep) the Law, was a clear statement of solidarity with these people. It was the prophet or rabbi extending the hand of friendship and peace by his sharing a rite that joined all in brotherhood. Jesus reached out actively to those in need, and the mere fact of eating with sinners spoke eloquently of acceptance and forgiveness.

Jesus also taught at meals. He used them especially to teach about God's mercy. The three parables of mercy in Luke 15 follow the complaint by those learned in the Law that "This man welcomes sinners and eats with them." During meals, Jesus would often heal or openly forgive sins and speak of the quality of God's love and compassion. Thus Jesus literally gave himself at these times, not only his personal presence, but his teaching and his complete willingness to do whatever was necessary to reconcile people to the Father.

If we look at the Last Supper, the meal so directly related to our Eucharist, we see Jesus using bread and wine, signs of the joy and plenty of the promised land. We know from the Qumran and other documents that bread and wine were reminders of God's bounty and protection, and his willingness—even eagerness—to deliver his people. They were fruits of the promised land. The one who presided at the festive meal prayed at the beginning, thus sharpening the symbolic value, and making the entire meal so sacred that latecomers were excluded. For, those who shared the bread and wine received a personal share in the blessing which had been spoken. One did not come just for the food. Jesus followed a somewhat similar pattern in his meals, and at the Last Supper focused the meaning of the sharing even more sharply by stating that the bread was his body and the wine his blood, the true blood of the new and everlasting covenant promised by Jeremiah (31:31-34).

These words have come to be known as words of

consecration. They were more than that. In a larger sense, they were actually words of *interpretation*, interpreting the true meaning of that meal, pointing out the significance of his life and the meaning of his death. Their value comes from the fact that they are undergirded and supported by a life of total self-giving, a death that was truly for others in order that they might live. Having loved his own who were in the world, he showed on the cross the full extent of his love. It was his life of complete selflessness that lets us know that his body is truly given for us and his blood shed on our behalf.

Hence, we can see that a deeper understanding of the values of a meal highlights several important points. The first is the forgiveness and reconciliation implied. A second is the notion of solidarity—the love and friendship that bind together those at the same table. A third is the sacrificial dimension which Jesus gave to our meal of fellowship. If we truly *do* in his memory what he did, we will be living a life focused on others as his was. A closer look at each of these points is necessary.

Jesus came that we might have life and have it in great abundance and, in reconciling us with the Father, he has brought us the forgiveness of our sins. When we think of forgiveness of sins today, we automatically tend to think of the sacrament of reconciliation, or penance. In no way wanting to diminish the proper place of this sacrament, it is a fact (one even mentioned in the instruction on the new rite of reconciliation) that the chief means of reconciliation in the church is the Eucharist.

To think of the Eucharist as being reconciliatory is

more than emphasizing the penitential rite at the beginning. It is saying that the whole meal, the entire Mass, is reconciliatory. Forgiveness is implied by the very fact that Jesus invites us to his table. All we need do is accept the invitation. This is where we see the tremendous compassion of God. Jesus' custom of eating with sinners was clearly meant to symbolize the goal of the messianic banquet: union of sinful humanity with God. At the Last Supper and in the Eucharist, Jesus makes explicit the meaning of his life and the message of all his earthly meals: This was how he would destroy the barriers between sinners and God.

We should reflect seriously on the fact that Jesus did not limit his meal fellowship to those who were already his disciples, or who were already "good." Zacchaeus is but one example of how Jesus reached beyond those considered "saved" to eat with one who was, in all probability, the biggest thief in town, to say nothing of his being in the employ of the Romans. The result of this expression of love and forgiveness was enough to move Zacchaeus to make restitution with interest and to give half of his goods to the poor. Jesus' gesture, his reaching out, was not only an expression of human good will, it was an extension of God's own acceptance; it was as such that Zacchaeus and those who sneered understood it, and it was undoubtedly this which moved him to repentance (see Lk 19:1-10).

The forgiveness implied in a meal, and especially in Christ's meal with us is now symbolized in the revised rite of the Eucharist. Following the Our Father, where we ask to be forgiven as we forgive others, we have a rite of peace where, before we share at the table of the Lord, we are asked to extend the hand of friendship and peace to those with whom we have been invited to Christ's table. This seemingly innocent ritual is one which is still omitted by some, and disliked by still others. It seems to intrude into our sacred space at a time when we are getting ready to receive the Lord.

What this gesture is trying to tell us, however, is that unless we are willing to extend the hand of peace to all with whom we are joined, our forgiveness and outreach are less than Jesus'. We are changing the nature of his meal from one of reconciliation and forgiveness to a private fantasy world where we are all alone with our Savior. But, Jesus has invited others to his table also; he cares for them as he does for us, and asks us to do likewise. If we cannot do this, we do not belong there; we are arbitrarily restricting God's love and contradicting the very meaning of our sharing at the same table.

Perhaps this may help us to pray better that deeply eucharistic prayer, the Our Father. When we ask to be forgiven as we forgive others, what are we really saying? Do we really want God to be no more generous and understanding of us than we are, at times, with others? Aside from the various spiritual interpretations that have been given this petition, it also seems to express simple basic psychology. If we restrict the meaning of forgiveness and solidarity in our own lives, if we harden our hearts to the outstretched hands of others, we so narrow our horizons that we are unable to benefit from the forgiveness which God is only too ready to offer. God's forgiveness does not depend on our own, but if our minds and hearts are so closed to what real forgiveness is, we do not recognize or accept the invitation or the grace when it is offered.

Solidarity is another element of Christian life that is inherent in understanding the meal aspects of Eucharist. It is baptism, surely, which has brought us into Christ's family in the first place. "Children of God and heirs of heaven" was the way it used to be expressed. And the various sayings in the Gospel about hating parents, family and friends for the sake of the kingdom stress the idea that Jesus has come to forge new bonds among people, bonds that go beyond family, tribe or nation (see Lk 14:26). He envisages a society where all can live together in peace and friendship. This is what he symbolized still further in choosing a meal during which to sacramentalize his presence and his meaning for the new family he hoped to form.

If we are to continue the work that Jesus has started, if our eucharistic celebrations are to reflect the actuality of our lives, we must learn to extend our reach beyond its present limits. Frequent sharing at the Lord's table should fill us with a desire to bring all men and women within the range of Christ's action. It means not being blinded by the sociological homogeneity of our present parish structures. Most cities have many parishes set up along geographical or sometimes national lines. This means we might never rub elbows with those from different classes or groups even within the same city, let alone our brothers and sisters in other countries.

Jesus, however, has only one table, to which all are called. We cannot so isolate ourselves that we feel no concern for others whom we may never meet. These "others" fall into two classes. The most obvious class consists of those who already share life in Christ. They are members of the family. But there are also those outside still waiting to be called to the Lord's table, people who—unless we reach out to them as Jesus did to Zacchaeus—may never experience the compassion of a loving Christ. We who share at Jesus' table are expected to extend his concern and love to all who need it.

Our challenge is such that the sacrificial aspects of a life lived for others should be abundantly clear. Jesus' own life of meal fellowship demonstrates his willingness to meet us in love, not a self-centered love, but one surpassing all limitation. His self-emptying down to and including his death on a cross is the example we have been given to follow. It is what we celebrate in the Eucharist. It is what we are expected to live ourselves.

Yet, it is more than just a challenge, a goal worth aiming for. It is at the heart and center of the meals we share with Jesus. If we are striving to live not for ourselves but for others, if we are truly trying to replace an innate selfishness with the concern and charity of Christ, then we are celebrating an effort to make our lives one with what is expressed liturgically. Without a life of genuine concern for others as demonstrated by Jesus, our celebrations become but empty words and meaningless actions.

In the struggle to better appreciate what the Eucharist means and implies, focusing on the meal aspects can be very fruitful. Rooted in our own appreciation of special and festive meals, we can perceive how Jesus built on the same foundation to express his own and God's love for us. We can see how he used meals as a characteristic element of his ministry, and how the Eucharist itself embodies all the values of outreach, of reconciliation and forgiveness, of solidarity and sacrificial love.

If we are to continue celebrating this reality sacramentally, our participation will be fruitful only to the extent that it mirrors and reflects a personal effort to enshrine the same values and attitudes in our own lives. Eucharist was never meant to reinforce a narrow spirituality that has no room for others. Rather, Jesus sits us down at table with a motley assortment of people and expects us to enjoy ourselves and to be at home.

VII

BREAD BROKEN AND SHARED

The film might have been entitled "Christmas Dinner in the Dump." Being homemade, however, it was untitled. But it was about real people, and it was all about Christmas in the town dump. We were being told of the apostolic efforts of some Jesuits working in El Paso, Texas. It seems that across the border from El Paso lies Juarez. Juarez is much better known to Americans for its cheap goods, its gambling and the other amenities provided by Mexican border towns. Less well known is the town dump, which dozens of people call home. There they build their shanties, raise their families and compete with the rats for the food that is provided daily by the garbage pails of the nearby city.

One of the Jesuits working with a group of cursillistas had gotten the brilliant idea of expressing something of the joy and peace of Christ's birthday by sharing Christmas dinner with the unfortunate people, the refuse of society, living—*existing* would be a better word—across the border. It was considered to be a good idea, so two dozen or so people with their families prepared food and gifts and set off for the dump on Christmas afternoon. They were not prepared for what they saw. Instead of the dozens which they expected to find, there were hundreds. They were completely outnumbered by the wretched poor whose only hope of survival was vying with others to glean the leftovers and discarded items of the city.

The film captured that so graphically: a small group laden with food advancing amid the garbage and rubble being met by an army of hungry for whom the available food would hardly be enough for appetizers. But they continued on and bravely told the people of their love and concern, and offered apologies that they had not brought sufficient food so that they might all enjoy a good Christmas dinner together. However, they could at least share as much as would go around. So, with songs, hymns and good will the dinner was begun. They took the food, blessed it, and distributed it to the people. Did they eat! The film showed smiling faces and full plates. The film also showed, inexplicably, that horde of humanity completely satisfied—and plenty of food left over. Once again the disciples gathered what was left over after all had had their fill. Once again, the Lord had wondrously fed the multitudes.

When we consider individual incidents in the life of Jesus, it is so easy to get lost on peripheral questions. When Jesus fed the multitude with a few fish and barley loaves, for example, we exercise ourselves over whether Jesus actually *multiplied* the bread and the fish, or whether people were simply motivated to share what little they had (a far greater miracle, incidentally), thus providing more than enough for all. The real issue is that Jesus, in his love and compassion, is able to provide for our needs, and has given us the means to satisfy them. This generosity of his is, furthermore, not limited to an isolated incident in his life; it is meant as a continuing reality in the life of the church. The real question is: How do people continue to be fed today?

We have already mentioned that from the earliest days, the incidents of the miraculous feeding in the life of Christ were presented as a eucharistic event. The liturgical actions of Jesus *taking* bread, *blessing* it, *breaking* it and *distributing* it, are found in all six accounts (Mk 6:41; Mk 8:6; Mt 14:19; Mt 15:36; Lk 9:16; Jn 6:11). Scripture scholars are even able to analyze the subtle changes in wording in the various texts, and see how they reflect the changing eucharistic practice of the early church. It is commonly agreed that the earliest efforts to understand and appreciate the meaning of the Eucharist in the early church attached this mystery to the feeding of the multitude long before evolving the liturgical narratives of the Last Supper. St. John, in fact, uses this as the major sign in Jesus' life which explains the meaning of Eucharist in the church. He gives no equivalent liturgical development to the Last Supper.

What made this possible was not only the value and meaning of meals in the ministry of Jesus—they were times when he shared freely of his teaching, his compassion, his forgiveness, his very self—but the special values inherent in feeding the huge multitude. They saw that this miraculous feeding prefigured their

Eucharist, could be used to convey important aspects of its nature, and offered continued guidance for the life of the church.

Thinking of the multiplication of loaves in this way perhaps does not come easy for us. When we think of the signs of the Eucharist, we generally limit them to the consecrated bread and wine. But the sign goes beyond the simple elements of food and drink. It extends to the entire giving event which Jesus initiated and made possible. The sign of the Eucharist lies in the human experience of a meal wherein is accomplished Jesus' ability to feed and nourish. It is an experience of friendship and community. It is a mystery of love and compassion. Because all these elements are found in the multiplication incident, it was natural for our forebears in the faith to look to it for meaning and purpose.

Jesus broke the bread. Bread is broken in order to be shared. And in sharing the same bread, all are made one. The shared bread helps forge the unity of those who partake of it. This sign of the Eucharist is a sign of solidarity, of fraternity. It is the bread which is broken and the wine which is shared which is always mentioned in the Scriptures. It is not the bread as such—that can be static—it is the broken bread, broken in a gesture that means solidarity and sharing.

We might ask ourselves three questions, all of which are interrelated. First of all, who are to be regarded as the beneficiaries of Christ's sharing? Then, what are the exigencies of the solidarity inherent in Eucharist? Finally, how is Christ's bread to be broken for a new world in our day?

If we focus first on the question of who is the

brother or sister for whom Christ's bread is to be broken, the Scriptures are quick to expand our horizons. One of the very interesting passages in St. Matthew's Gospel speaks about the last judgment (25:31-46). Contrary to common expectation, God does not appear as a bookkeeper judge having catalogued all our sins against the commandments. The commandments, in fact, are not mentioned at all. Rather, we are told, salvation hinges on the positive efforts we have made to reach out to those in need: to give food and drink to the hungry, to comfort the afflicted, to visit the sick and imprisoned, etc. The reason is that whenever we reach out to the poor, to the least of Christ's brethren, we touch Christ himself. It is not sufficient to do nothing wrong; we are expected to do right, to work for justice, to build a Christlike world.

We sometimes feel that we have made great strides when we make the effort to recognize Christ in the person of all the baptized. It is true that he dwells within them and that we have neglected this presence for too long, but the Scriptures tell us to go further still. Both Matthew's judgment parable as well as Luke, when he recalls the parable of the good Samaritan (10:29-37), take us beyond the narrow confines of our own religious household. By bringing a Samaritan into this latter story, Jesus defines neighborliness as the ability to show love. Jesus reverses the question asked him by the lawyer to insist that the real question is not who is one's neighbor, but how can one be a good neighbor to those in need. Jesus' bread must be broken and shared.

There is no doubt, if we reflect on these parables, that in some strange and wondrous manner, the faces of the poor reflect the face of the suffering Christ. It is the element of humanity with which Jesus freely identified. Jesus took upon himself the lot of the poor, the sinners, those who cried out to him in need. In the poor, then, we are able to see those of our brethren with whom Jesus most closely identified. If the incarnation—God's taking up human flesh—means anything, it means that God revealed himself not in suburbia, but on the wrong side of the tracks.

In his own suffering and death, Jesus took upon himself the lot of the poor, of those alienated by sin. He was willingly wounded for our transgressions, because we did not have the power to change our own situation. This is what we memorialize each time we celebrate Eucharist. And so, if our participation is to be real, we must grow to love, serve and listen to those in need, knowing that in so doing we identify ourselves with the mysterious intention of Christ. We join him in the most practical aspect of his incarnation and redemption.

Entering into the service of humankind, promoting human welfare and the works of justice in any way whatever are part of the work of the Gospel. This is not to say that we can find in Scripture a particular social doctrine; however, we do find therein the principle of loving one another as we ourselves have been loved, a hardheaded concrete love of all whom the Bible calls "neighbor." Our charity, like that of Christ, should reflect the compassion of God, and should be idealistic yet realistic enough to aim at the reduction and elimination of every kind of human misery.

This implies more than that Christians should involve themselves for others. Social action of itself is insufficient. But if we understand Eucharist as the mystery of Christ's continuing ability to feed his people, if we know that his bread is broken to be shared with the needy and the poor, this will form our attitude and lend the dynamism of faith to our efforts. We need a clear ideal of what kind of world we are striving to build, and the ideal we take from the Lord's table is that he has given us brothers and sisters the world over who have a claim on us because we accept the bread broken in order to be shared. If we truly believe that Christ is the life and the hope of the world, if our gathering about the altar is truly a proclamation of new bonds and relationships made possible only in Christ, this consciousness should permeate our concern as well as our efforts to build a better world. Engaged in the task of lessening the world's misery or in the more positive struggle to improve the quality of life in our cities and towns, we should be a eucharistic people. We not only celebrate that point to which we hope to lead others, we work to make it a reality. The reality is not just a better world, it is a vision of the true meaning of life, the meaning given it by Jesus when he fed the multitude, the meaning we celebrate in Eucharist.

A perspective like this one is necessary, because of the difficulties involved, if we are to avoid an ethereal rose-water type of piety. We can speak of love, but never do anything to spread it. As Linus (of *Peanuts* fame) once remarked, "Humanity I love; it's people I can't stand." Talk of seeing Christ in others, or of being reconciled to all, demands effort. It goes beyond the sweet smile that says, "I love the Christ in you," when the person himself is in need of love. We must avoid giving the impression that we're interested in others only "because we see Christ in them," thus effectively wrapping the whole world in a blessed anonymity.

Furthermore, the solidarity and reconciliation implied in meals does not imply a society or community where all differences are erased, where there is always sweet unanimity, or where dissenting voices or opinions no longer exist. The communion intended by Christ does not cover over human differences and conflicts, it *transcends* them. Reconciliation is not veneer. We recognize that we have found in Jesus a deeper source of unity, a purposeful life to which we can commit ourselves, and a common goal which can unite us all: universal brotherhood.

There is no need for developing a "least common denominator" approach to life, either. Out of misguided respect for the liberty and freedom of others, we can wind up doing nothing. A truly adult community would better work for consensus, but a consensus based on life in Christ, as we remember his willingness to feed the hungry, a feeding that was based simply on need, not on whether people were attractive, or otherwise appealing. But if all who share the Lord's table would truly enter into the action of Jesus, and try to express this for one another, the world would soon become a community of reconciliation, mercy and peace. All that is required is the ability to pause and focus attention on the source of our bread, of our life.

These reflections simply follow a perspective already sketched out for us in the accounts of the feeding of the multitude. A tradition that is evident in most of the accounts stresses the involvement of the disciples in Jesus' action. In the first place, they inform

Jesus of the people's hunger and are told that they should give the people something to eat themselves. At this point all they can do is protest that they do not have enough. They are unaware of both their responsibility and their ability.

But when Jesus said the blessing over the little that was available, he again involved the disciples by giving them the food to distribute. They were also in charge of collecting the fragments that were left over. Jesus' bread is broken, but it will be shared only if there are sufficient disciples to distribute the benefits of Christ's bounty.

The early church was only too aware that it could not look backward forever to the past work of Jesus; it had to shoulder the responsibility he had left it. For Jesus' memorial to be truly meaningful and effective, the disciples knew that they must give continuous expression to his attitude, word and action. In this way a historically significant action could be given ever-new life in liturgical celebrations which reflected the ongoing practice of the community.

We all need the early Christians' awareness that the risen Christ continues to work through us. The task of assessing the needs and resources of the hungry is assigned to the disciples down through the ages, as is the task of distributing the nourishment that Jesus continues to make possible. We are asked to assume Jesus' own attitude of self-giving each time we celebrate Eucharist. We are all challenged to make Christ's eucharistic words our own and to give of ourselves as he did. We are called to proclaim that our search for brotherhood has its foundation in Jesus' own life, in his own self-gift.

BREAD BROKEN AND SHARED

Christians have a need to celebrate not simply the past mystery of Jesus, or the memory of the risen Lord, but the daily presence of Christ in the life of the church. For the Eucharist is not just a source of grace enabling us to live our Christian lives. We are enclosed and included in what we celebrate. The more authentic our commitment to mission, to sharing the broken bread, the more will Christ's presence be recognized.

The incident in Juarez with which we began this chapter is real. It is today. It highlights the fact that God's wondrous deeds need not be things of the past. It also illustrates that it is only when Christians are alive enough to their responsibility that the power of Christ's grace will ever go beyond the confines of church to touch the lives of people. This takes faith and it takes courage. But if our celebrations are real, we will know that Christ has broken the bread and shared with us, and is only looking for us to do likewise.

VIII

THE DEMANDS OF EUCHARIST

One of the obvious trends in the church today is the growing number of Catholics who seldom celebrate the Sunday Eucharist. Some countries are notorious for the large percentage of baptized who rarely give external expression to faith. Even in the United States, it seems, despite the numerous changes since the Vatican Council, there has not been a resultant rush to fill the churches. Meanwhile, the Council boldly proclaimed that the Eucharist is the source and summit of Christian life. How is it that there is such a disparity between theory and practice?

If we ask what common understanding most people have of the Eucharist, we would find that most practicing Catholics probably fit in one of the following classes:

A large number of Catholics show up at church on Sunday out of a sense of obligation. They are there because church law tells them to be there and because they do not want to flirt with mortal sin. Many in this group sit in back, seldom participate actively, and leave as soon as they can. They do not really involve themselves, and while they generally favor the liturgical changes, their own lives have not really been affected as a result. Since their main motivation for being in church is external, were the law on Sunday obligation to change, we would seldom see these people at church again.

Another group regularly attends Mass on Sundays because such practice is reinforced by the accepted norms of family or society. This is still the case in many smaller communities, especially if there is a strong ethnic population there. It's not so much that it is the accepted thing to do on Sundays, for most of these accept the tradition unquestioningly. But even those who might question the value of regular church affiliation and attendance are kept in line by group and family expectations. Because it is especially the social mores of the group that form the basis for participation, we don't always find that much active participation in this group either. These people arrive late and leave early, but they are generally satisfied with a traditional liturgy which does not vary week to week, and which allows them to return home afterwards to resume their ordinary lives.

Another sizeable group would not think of missing Mass on Sunday, because it truly is for them the high point of their devotional and religious life. Convinced that Jesus is really present in the Eucharist under the forms of bread and wine, all their prayers converge here as that point where Jesus is the closest to them. These people participate better than the previous two groups, although many are busy with their own prayers and devotions which they pursue while Mass is going on. It is a sacred time for them, and it reinforces their attachment to Jesus just to be there. Those who do participate, however, are even more involved, have a strong sense of duty, and are generally serious Catholics.

Yet a final group who are good and active participants see the Eucharist as God's greatest gift to us. Born from the love of Christ as he offered his life for us, it is a testament of his grace and service. It is the greatest of the sacraments and the chief source of grace in the church as in one's personal life. Regular participation, often including daily Mass, characterizes many in this group, who are eager to join themselves to this mysterious source of life and love which God has provided. It is an action that puts them in contact with the transcendent God, and one that satisfies the soul's desire for union.

These groupings obviously say little or nothing to those who seldom darken the doors of the church. The wry jokes used to speak of "hatched, matched and dispatched" Catholics. But whether these people appear on major feast days or on the occasion of weddings and funerals, the Eucharist is largely irrelevant to their lives. Many of them would fight to the death to insist on their Catholicity. It remains true, nevertheless, that sacramental participation holds almost no meaning for them and is totally divorced from their daily lives.

The real problem here is not so much the ability to categorize ourselves or others but, rather, why have we come to this pass? It is too simplistic to blame the liturgical changes which have taken place. Polls have shown that the vast majority of Catholics are quite happy with the changes. It cannot be denied, however, that changing the altars and using the vernacular has eliminated a certain sense of mystery and exposed the Mass for what it actually is, in all its glory as well as in its weaknesses. It is not a question either of assessing blame, but rather of trying to determine whether or not our own attitude about the Eucharist helps reinforce the existing situation. Surely, if change is to come, it will have to come from us; it will come from the bottom and the ability which small groups of committed Christians have to change the world.

If we look at the attitudes mentioned so far in this chapter, they all have one thing in common: They are *passive*. In each of them, the Eucharist is something which happens to us. It is either a liturgical action at which we assist or, even better, in which we participate, or it is a source of grace, inspiration and union with Christ. But it rarely ever becomes *our* action. It is a sacred ritual which we trace back to Jesus, but one whose form, content and expression have little input from the community. Be it America or Africa, Europe or Latin America, the Eucharist is the same. Be it time of war or famine, peace or prosperity, the Mass has remained unchanged in its essentials for centuries. We are expected to plug into a ritual which is valid for all times; and, by and large, most of us feel that this is normal and the way things should be and were meant to be by Jesus himself.

This was not the way the Eucharist was intended by Christ, nor the way it was seen by the early church. Rather, it was intimately associated with the early

Christians' understanding of baptism—as outlined in the first chapter—and was an *active* celebration of their adult responsibility to join their lives with that of Christ for the salvation of the world. Let us review some of the New Testament material on the Eucharist, making an effort, however, to be active rather than passive in our point of view.

Recall once again Jesus' response to James and John when they asked for places of honor in his kingdom. Good teacher that he was, Jesus did not refuse them outright or even tell them how mistaken they were. Rather, he used the occasion to teach just what being first in the kingdom implied: "Can you drink the cup that I must drink or be baptized with the baptism with which I must be baptized?" (Mk 10:38). Jesus links the cup which he himself will drink with baptism and with his sacrificial death. This is the cup whose contents were further specified at the Last Supper as his blood, "the blood of the covenant, which is to be poured out for many" (Mk 14:24), and in which the disciples all shared.

It was the same cup which Jesus was tempted to avoid in the garden when he prayed that it be taken from him, if at all possible (Mk 14:36), but which he eventually drained to the dregs on the cross. In the same way was his body broken for us. The liturgy interprets and explains the meaning of Jesus' redemptive death so well: "During the meal he took bread, blessed and broke it, and gave it to them. 'Take it,' he said, 'This is my body.... This is my blood, the blood of the covenant, which is to be poured out for many' " (Mk 14:22, 24). The Eucharist in which we share is truly a sharing in the death of Christ.

83

BREAD BROKEN AND SHARED

But is this sharing meant to be only something which we receive, which is given for us, or is it something which we also give? Is it only something which we benefit from, or is it something that we join in offering? Surely we have always thought of it as something which we receive. The mode of giving Communion reinforces this: We stick out our hand or our tongue and the Eucharist is given to us with the words, "Body (and blood) of Christ." Even the priest concentrates especially on what he is receiving in the prayer which the liturgy puts on his lips: "May the body (and blood) of Christ bring my soul to everlasting life." This is not the perspective of Mark, who understands sharing as joining actively with Christ. That is what is asked of all who share Christ's life and mission in baptism; it is also what we are always tempted to avoid.

When the Christian disciple in the garden who is attempting to follow Jesus is threatened, like Christ, with imprisonment, torture and death, he abandons his noble ideals and flees away naked, as the other disciples had already done (Mk 14:50-52). When Simon of Cyrene, known as the father of two of the early Christians, was given the opportunity to shoulder the cross of Christ, he had to be forced to do so. The opportunities which these people missed are the opportunities which are offered us each time we celebrate anew the sacrifice of Christ. Seen in this way, it is possible to see the Eucharist from the point of view of *giving* more than receiving. Our challenge is to freely accept that cross, to willingly drink that cup, and to make Jesus' words and actions our own. We are happy to be and to live as Christians!

THE DEMANDS OF EUCHARIST

Perhaps one of the main reasons why so many Christians are left cold by the Eucharist is that we have succeeded in divorcing Christ's actions from our own. Rather than each eucharistic celebration being an expression and celebration of the community's commitment to live for others and to give of itself for the life of the world, it becomes simply a recalling of Christ's own life apart from any ongoing effect from his body, the church. If the loud proclamation that "This is the cup of my blood which will be shed for you" refers only to Christ, Eucharist becomes essentially an exercise in historical memory.

When those words are made our own, however, when they reflect a life of service and of self-giving inspired by and made possible only by Jesus, then the Eucharist becomes extremely meaningful each time that it is celebrated because it is a visible continuation of Christ's salvation. Instead of a Eucharist which seems more a ritual celebration of a group with no real message for or commitment to the world in which we live, it becomes a bold proclamation of that same community's concern for others. Our memorial of Christ's sacrifice is something into which we have entered personally; we have made his words and actions our own.

It is the Catholic temptation to reduce the signs of Jesus' eucharistic presence to the bread and the wine. We have long been taught that these elements are transformed and become the actual body and blood of the Lord. And so we have tabernacles before which we pray and to which we offer reverence. For the early church, however, it was especially Christ's sacrificial *action* that was being memorialized ("*Do* this in remembrance of me," Jesus said. We were not challenged simply to repeat his words, or institute a ritual action; we were asked to do as he did, to offer our lives that others might live).

The signs of the Eucharist go beyond the bread and wine. They are the bread which is broken and shared, the wine poured out in reconciliation; the entire giving-event signifies Christ's eucharistic gift. If Jesus is the only one doing the giving, if the rest of the community is wrapped up in selfish isolation, with hands out only to receive rather than give, we are stripping the Eucharist of all real meaning; we are reducing it to an impoverished ritual.

It is far easier, surely, to focus on Jesus in the bread and wine. For that allows us to be passive; we can concentrate mostly on what Jesus is doing for us. As recipients we need not concern ourselves especially about others. Eucharistic action is entirely on the part of Christ toward us. If it is the entire giving-event which is important, however, if it is the whole Christ, head and members, who are part of the action, then it is our very persons which become part of the sacramental sign. Experientially, this is a far more living and actual sign of Christ's presence in our world than what passes for Eucharist in most of our churches.

This approach, which is surely that of the early Christians, orients all the participants away from concern with their own lives toward the giving of life to others. Eucharist thus strengthens and reaffirms the basic baptismal commitment of living and dying for others. Appreciated in this way, Eucharist prevents us from being complacent and closing our eyes to those conditions around us which prevent people from really living. There is no way we can repeatedly celebrate Eucharist, renewing our commitment to live and die for others, and not reach out to the poor and oppressed as Jesus did. The concern for justice, and seeing to it that the Eucharist is truly bread broken for a new world of brotherhood and peace, lies in our hands. If we do not concern ourselves for others in this way, our eucharistic celebrations are little more than an empty mouthing of words whose meaning is long since forgotten. Worse still, our celebration is a lie.

If we mourn and wonder why Catholics are less interested in celebrating Eucharist these days, the reason just might be that, aware of all the implications of sharing in Christ's memorial, they are not yet ready for that level of commitment. It is more likely that they do not feel challenged by an active sense of commitment on the part of those who do celebrate the Eucharist. If the churches are filled only with people there to receive for themselves, it can seem like a corporate exercise of selfishness about which there is little that is attractive. If, on the other hand, Eucharist is the obvious expression of an ongoing Christian gift of self, if it celebrates the willingness to place our lives on the line for others, it will become a living reality, pulsating with a spirit of Christlike concern for others. This will attract others; life always does.

Although it would be easy (and in some places easier than others!) to say that, unless the structures of church and parish change, the active celebration which characterized the early church is impossible today, this is begging off responsibility. There are three stages in which change can come.

The first requires that our own attitude to the celebration of Eucharist change from passive to active. That will force us to root out of our own lives whatever militates against social justice. We can no longer sit back and do nothing about injustice or societal structures which perpetuate poverty and oppression. We will become involved.

That will naturally cause us to join with others, not only in some form of social apostolate, but in prayer and celebration. The Eucharist will provide both a focus and a measure for continued growth and commitment, besides challenging us to specific action and concern. Knowing others of like mind makes the effort easier and prevents discouragement.

Finally, if we are at all concerned about the larger parish, we must work to incorporate this vision into the whole. If the Eucharist is ever seen as the celebration of an active continuous concern for others, one won't have to worry about the peripheral changes ordinarily associated with liturgical renewal. The interior change will be so great and so obvious that everything else will fall into line.

IX

INDIVIDUALISM: THE MODERN HERESY

Heresy usually involves doctrines or practices contrary to the truth of Catholic faith. In singling out individualism for that dubious honor, we do not mean to imply that it is a new phenomenon which threatens to disrupt the peace of the religious scene. However, since the Vatican Council we are becoming aware of new directions and approaches to God, and many older trends are found to be wanting. One of them—individualism—strikes at the heart of the current understanding of church and Eucharist. Since it is firmly ensconced in our past practice, however, we are being asked to look clearly at ourselves to see to what extent we are invited to change our practice.

The problem is compounded because there is no question here of "good guys versus bad guys"; people on both sides are usually very sincere. It is the age-old dilemma of spirituality. The basic question is: What does it mean to live a full Christlike life; what does it mean to be "holy"? One end of the spectrum sees the answer as involving a refined religiosity which includes prayer, meditation, reflection on Scripture and personal union with Christ, especially in the Eucharist. In short, it involves a religious idealism which seeks to rise above temporal concerns and the entanglements of the world to that area where the soul can be alone to commune with God. The opposite end of the spectrum sees the correct solution as requiring that faith in Jesus means a life totally committed to living here and now, in this place, and in this world. It means being involved.

Obviously, these are caricatures; but the tendencies reveal themselves, for example, in what people expect of priestly ministry. "Priests should give us God and nothing more," some say. "They should confine themselves to their spiritual ministry, and not bring politics, social action or economics into the pulpit." Whether we spontaneously agree with this or not is a good indication of what we instinctively feel is the proper role of the priest and the place which the Eucharist has in our lives.

We may be wrong.

We are still in a period of change following the Vatican Council. This change involves not only practice but theory. During the Council the church was able to look at itself calmly and try to discern where the Holy Spirit was leading it. The resultant changes of emphasis in pastoral and dogmatic theology, despite their far-reaching importance, were dwarfed, however (as far as most people were concerned), by the liturgical changes that came shortly after the Council. The mere fact of returning to a vernacular liturgy reversed over 1,600 years of Latin sway. Strangely, when Greek was replaced with Latin in the Western church at the end of the fourth century, the various European languages were already beginning their development. The common faithful were increasingly burdened with incomprehensible language, rites and symbolism. Their ability to participate intelligently in liturgy and the life of the church grew less and less. We are all the heirs of a long period of unenlightened practice and devotion. It will take years to change what needs changing.

This seemingly harsh judgment must be nuanced, of course. What it means in practice is that we should all examine our presuppositions and practice to see to what extent they measure up to sound theology. We need not delve into the long history behind present eucharistic piety; we should be aware, however, whether there are discrepancies between the solid tradition of the church, its present teaching and our own attitudes and practice. There is no doubt that in the early centuries, the Eucharist was the corporate religious expression of the entire Christian community. Somewhere along the line—and the mechanics of the process are not important—the Eucharist degenerated from the most solemn and authentic communal expression of the Lord's dominion over his church into a private devotion. This, in turn, fostered individualistic piety which is at odds with the theology of Vatican II.

Pope John Paul II underscores this also in the letter he wrote on the Eucharist for Holy Thursday (1980). After stating that the church is brought into being through union of people, through the experience of brotherhood to which the eucharistic banquet gives

91

rise, he goes on to state that the Eucharist will only be the "source and summit" of Christian life if the Eucharist is rightly conceived. "The church is brought into being when, in fraternal union and communion, we celebrate the sacrifice of the cross of Christ, when we proclaim 'the Lord's death until he comes,' and later, when, being deeply compenetrated with the mystery of our salvation, we approach as a community the table of the Lord, in order to be nourished there, in a sacramental manner, by the fruits of the holy sacrifice of propitiation. Therefore, in eucharistic communion we receive Christ, Christ himself; and our union with him, which is a gift and grace for each individual, brings it about that in him we are also associated in the unity of his body which is the church" (#4).

Throughout this book, tremendous emphasis has been placed on the community aspects of Christianity and of eucharistic piety. The concern is that in many places the Eucharist is not seen in this way. What is meant to be the authentic expression of community has become detached from that community. The mere fact that it is not generally regarded as a force which challenges us to fight for right or to involve ourselves in the social sphere is a case in point. The bread which is broken should impel us to work for the creation of a new world. All too often Christ's sacrifice has become a private devotion, seen essentially as a source of personal grace independently of any involvement with the larger Christian community.

Perhaps the clearest witness to the fact that this is indeed the case is the extent to which most Catholics view the Mass as a sacred inviolable ritual. There were (and continue to be) major debates over each minor issue of liturgical reform. Much heat was generated over such things as the change in position of the altar, the language used, the type of music or instruments used, posture, Communion kneeling or standing, Communion in the hand, or under both species. Even a seemingly innocuous change in the Eucharistic Prayer to say that Christ's blood was shed for women as well as all men has strong partisans pro and con. Indeed, the fact that Catholics could be divided over such issues in the past 20 years is significant. Seldom even mentioned are the fundamental missionary and community dimensions of Eucharist. That these questions and those of societal changes needed to build a new world in Christ are given only secondary treatment, if any at all, means that they are strangely irrelevant to the worshiping community.

Yet, when the Eucharist, which is supposed to be the most solemn and authentic celebration of the sacrifice of Christ, becomes cult or private devotion, we are witnessing a profound deterioration in religious sensitivity. From the beginning, the eucharistic celebration was conceived of only in concelebration of the entire community. The breakdown came when people began to regard the liturgy as a collection of practices intended for the salvation of the individual. If one's main fear was eternal damnation, it was a logical jump to conclude that the most effective means of obtaining the graces of salvation was the Mass. And if one Mass was good, two were even better.

In this fashion, Eucharist became detached from the community to become the isolated object of private devotion. The emphasis on ritual requirements and the rigidity of structure that we have come to associate with the liturgy help give the impression that here is the most sacred moment of our day, the most efficacious way for personal sanctification. Especially for those who regard sanctity as an otherworldly reality that puts us in direct personal contact with the divine, the sacred aspects of liturgy reinforce the notion of the holy and transcendent. In this perspective, the ups and downs of life have really no place, and should not concern the truly "holy" person. In fact, all in society can come to the fount of grace which is the Eucharist, meet there, and go back to their respectively different lives and situations feeling justified and comforted in the Mass.

Many books and articles have supplied a pattern of reasons why and how this came to be. Suffice it to say that we have gone from a period when the Eucharist was recognized as the corporate public worship of the whole community to one where it is no longer generally regarded as the action of the people. Rather, it is seen as the action of God, through the intermediary of the priest. Primary emphasis is put on the worship of the Lord present in the host. Adoration began to replace sharing, and fear of God to overshadow a sense of loving partnership with him. The authentically objective and communitarian spirit of the liturgy ceded to a more subjective form of piety.

The consequences of this were particularly bad; switching the emphasis from the union of the whole church (and individuals as part of that church) with God to the union of individual souls with God alone led to an all-absorbing subjectivism. It left no room for the social dimension, and saw no intrinsic connection with our sharing at the Lord's table and a corresponding duty of building the kingdom in the world. People became more concerned with gaining grace and acquiring merit than with commitment to the mission of Christ in the world.

This eclipse of the doctrine that the whole church is the Body of Christ is partly responsible for the growth of individualism and subjectivism. Along with this was a similar change in the attitude of the church to Jesus Christ. In the early church, Jesus was seen as our elder brother, whose divine origin made it possible for us to pray to the Father through him. Ironically, all liturgical prayers are still couched in those terms. During the Middle Ages, however, focus shifted from regarding Jesus as one who gave the example which we should follow, one who was like us in all things but sin (Heb 4:15), to one who was essentially divine. This put far greater stress on worship, and less on fellowship; Jesus was to be adored in his sacrament more than followed in his sacrifice. The whole mission of Jesus as one who came to serve others rather than reign over them came to be forgotten. Years of prayer and worship could have absolutely no social consequences and be thought normal.

Today, however, we live in a different age. The Vatican Council's vision in large measure was a response to change in the very world in which we live. There is far more awareness now of the interdependence of nations, of the ecological consequences of our decisions and lifestyle. The recapturing of the early Christians' awareness of the interpersonal character of life and worship is essential if we are to have anything to say to the world. "But you are a chosen race, a royal priesthood, a consecrated nation, a people set apart to sing the praises of God who called you out of darkness into his wonderful light. Once you were not a people at all, and now you are the People of God" (1 Pt 2:9-10).

The task of this new people is twofold: both within and without the community. We are reminded of our interrelatedness by such reminders as "You should carry each other's troubles and fulfill the law of Christ" (Gal 6:2). Or, "Avoid getting into debt, except the debt of mutual love. If you love your fellowmen you have carried out your obligations" (Rom 13:8). The reason for this is simple: Having been baptized into one body in the Holy Spirit, "If one member suffers, all the members suffer with it; if one member is honored, all the members share its joy" (1 Cor 12:26). St. John reminds us of the extent of our concern, the example of Jesus himself: "This has taught us love—that he gave up his life for us; and we, too, ought to give up our lives for our brothers" (1 Jn 3:16). But our concern is not exclusively for the community; the community itself should be outgoing: "Love your neighbor" was never restricted to our own.

It is, as the church tells us over and over again, through the Eucharist that the communal nature of Christianity is best expressed and celebrated. For, of all the liturgical signs, the oldest and most important is the community itself. The church, the "people of God," is a reunion-in-worship made possible by God for the good of the participants and of the entire world. It is not just a collection of individuals who happen to be gathered in the same place. Surely the Eucharist which draws them together is the cause and sign of their unity. This sign, however, becomes piteously weak if the corporate dimensions are not seen and appreciated.

This is not to imply that, through the Eucharist, God bestows grace wholesale on the entire group. If individuals benefit, however, it is specifically as Christians whose vocation binds them up with a larger family which is part of their call. There are several questions which might help pinpoint our general orientation.

1. Is being a Catholic seen more as participation in a larger family or in terms of a direct relationship with God? Do grace and strength come by reason of the community, or directly from God?

2. Does Christianity require active participation of each individual in the group? Is community essential to Christianity or is it a luxury—nice when it's there, but really not necessary?

3. Does the church exist to bring salvation to the world, or more as a source of personal salvation? Is a social apostolate part and parcel of the nature of the church, or is it only a consequence which flows from union with Christ?

4. Should there be, ideally, a continuity between the economic or sociopolitical aspects of life and the liturgy, or should liturgical prayer be "above" the cares and concerns of everyday existence?

Obviously, the first half of each question espouses the communitarian view, while the last part is more individualistic. When St. Paul urged his converts to live "in Christ," a phrase which enters frequently in each epistle, he is not thinking of the mystical Christ in heaven or the eucharistic Christ on earth. He is speaking of the Body of Christ in the faithful, and insisting that the Christ-life is made possible only in and through a vital, caring Christian community whose example and support provide the environment for true conversion. This is what we are meant to celebrate at the altar.

This type of celebration will truly manifest the church for what it is. Any community gathered here and now is more than itself; the *more* comes from Christ and from a link to the universal church. The concern that should always surface to alleviate the suffering of humanity flows from identification with Jesus' own opposition to the evil powers that bind and oppress. If the Eucharist is to be an adequate symbol for the world today, as well as an effective force for building a more Christlike world, people will have to see that the bread which Jesus shares with us is not to be jealously hoarded, but freely shared with all in need.

X

HOW TO PRAY IN CHURCH

One of the complaints frequently made against a more activist or communitarian model of Eucharist is that it doesn't give us any real time for private prayer. Liturgical celebration no longer is a time of deep communion with God. The modern Mass, with its folksy emphasis on participation, seems to rule out any possibility of mystical experience.

What is the Christian prayer which Jesus has bequeathed us? How is this related to the Mass? The following story may help us understand. When my sister returned from five years of missionary work in New Caledonia, she spoke of one island where the natives were literally back in the stone age. There was no running water or electricity there, and the natives at one end of the mosquito-infested land had never traveled the 15 miles or so to get from one section of the island to the other. The natives, despite their common isolation from other lands, spoke two different languages and couldn't even understand one another. At one end there was an ancient tree, thought by the natives to belong to the god of the island and sacred to him alone. They were convinced that if they drew too close, or ever touched that tree, they would die. Despite the fact that the missionaries would climb all over it, when one native actually stumbled against it in a drunken state one night, the realization of what he had done was enough for him to promptly die of fright and heart attack.

How different from Jesus' teaching that God is not some awesome monster to be feared, but a loving father whom we should feel free to call by that name! The Aramaic word "*abba*," which Jesus himself always used and bequeathed to us, has all the loving familiarity of a child on its father's knee reaching out and saying, "daddy." This is the most basic and indispensable foundation of Christian prayer: God is not someone we need fear; he is a loving father.

Though some may have over-learned the lesson, and developed a carelessness that is alarming, many Catholics still harbor a pagan mentality toward God despite protests to the contrary. Those who fear God pray in quite similar ways. Three essentially pagan attitudes are that prayer is ritualistic, formalistic and repetitive. Certain prayers have to be recited in exactly the right words, with the correct gestures, or repeated a specified number of times in order to work. If all these conditions are met, the prayer has an almost automatic success ratio, a magic efficacy that is foolproof.

What makes this pagan is that the motivation behind it is largely fear and ignorance. Prayer is not a means of union with God; it is something to keep him in his place so he won't bother us. Using the prescribed rites (which he presumably wants) will prevent his being angry with us and, therefore, get us what we ask for. A secondary hope lurking in this sort of prayer is that it will somehow change God's mind. Correct prayer will prevail upon God to break down and grant us what he was not otherwise minded to give. We hardly have a picture of a loving father when we have to twist God's arm to get the amenities we need or want. God cannot be manipulated in this way.

There is a surprising residue of this mentality in many Catholic circles, however. Call it the "novena mentality." I remember once some upset woman rushing into the sacristy after a novena service because I had inadvertently changed a couple of words. She was afraid that spoiled the effectiveness of the prayer. But the novena mentality goes deeper than that. It manifests itself in the perennial popularity of chain prayers, or of people latching on to particular prayers as being especially worthwhile, or people who have a whole set of devotions they must "get in" each day, or those who see even Mass as the time to say the Rosary or some other personal prayers instead of participating in the prayer of Christ. Somehow the attitude persists that if we use the right words, or say them a magical number of times, God will finally come across and listen to us. Pure paganism!

To begin with the conviction that God is a loving father is not an insight we could develop on our own. It has been made possible only because God himself wanted to reveal it to us. It is something which we come to appreciate especially from Jesus' own life and teaching. Accepting and appreciating the fact that God is father not only shapes and influences the form and content of our prayer, it helps us to realize that true prayer is a gift of God. Prayer is not something we give to God, it is his own self-communication by which we are blessed. We need more of the attentive attitude of Samuel who, grateful to know at last that it was God himself who wished to communicate with him, answered simply, "Speak, Lord, your servant is listening." All too often our attitude seems to be, "Listen, Lord, your servant is speaking." We can speak nothing worthwhile that has not been granted us by our Father in heaven.

Recognizing God as Father, however, has definite consequences for life. As we see God revealed in the pages of Scripture, we come to know him better. We learn he has a name which must be kept holy, and a kingdom that must still be brought about. We recognize that we have been given a definite share in accomplishing this, for we accept his will as normative for us here on earth. It is ours to live out and fulfill. It is precisely in this that the greatness and dignity of Christian adulthood lies. Within the radical dependence which we have on God as author of life and grace and source of all good, we are able to situate the creative role he has destined for us. We know that mission flows from the very fact of being part of the family. Christians are not minors. Baptism and the commitment to Christ and our Father that is implied therein, requires that we look upon ourselves as adults. As such, our relationship to our father changes as we achieve greater maturity and purpose. God does not treat us as perpetual 5-year-olds; he wants and expects us to grow and to renew the face of the earth.

Because of the special place of Jesus, however, we can best learn what it means to be children of the Father by patterning our lives on his. He will ever remain not only the one who revealed God as Father, but one whose life was a perfect model of total obedience and fidelity. Jesus' effort to be faithful to his Father's will, to hallow his name and bring about his kingdom is revealed in his own prayer. From his prolonged desert retreat to his prayer in the garden before his final hour, one thought dominated: "Your will be done."

We see Jesus praying often throughout his public life. At all its turning points, prayer was what gave him understanding of the Father's will and the strength and courage to pursue it. Thus, before beginning his public life, before choosing the apostles, before his eucharistic teaching in John 6 and at his transfiguration, in preparation for the solemn moment of Peter's confession, and in preparation for his own teaching on prayer, as well as before undergoing the passion and death, Jesus prayed. This prayer was always made with the deep consciousness that his Father would hear him in his love; it was also concerned with mission.

When the Spirit came upon Jesus at his baptism in the Jordan, directing him to begin his own separate ministry, he spent 40 days in the desert to concern himself with one basic question: What did the Father want? What type of messiah would he be? We see him rejecting the easy, the typically human solutions, seeking only to be true to the Father's will as he was given to understand it. Not for him the path of compromise or of personal advantage. As in Gethsemane, he did not seek his own will. Jesus' refusal to escape the human condition he had accepted, and his unwillingness to call upon God to indulge his own pleasure, should be a lesson to all who would call upon God as Father. Jesus did not call upon the divine power simply to gratify immediate physical desires; he chose the ordinary way all of us must choose. He refused to rely on physical force, to crush heads and conquer enemies; he chose, rather, to stress the paramount importance of personal transformation and compassion in building the kingdom. He spurned cheap and spectacular signs and display; he chose instead unremitting personal effort and sacrifice. This was the Father's will.

Why could he decide this way? Because he knew God was a loving Father. To call God *Father* is to know that goodness is more powerful than evil, and that truth will overcome falsehood. To have a Father in heaven is to believe that in the end goodness and truth and the kingdom will triumph over all. Anyone who does not believe in God's ultimate victory is an atheist. There is a power and possibility for good in the world the way God made it, a power that, if freed, will be irresistible. Jesus believed this, and invited us to do likewise.

In this sense, we can see in the memorial of Jesus' redemptive suffering/death/resurrection the model of all true Christian prayer. For the Eucharist is the sacramental celebration of Jesus' voluntary annihilation for our sake in obedience to the Father's will. There we see and celebrate Jesus' gift to us and the glorification which he himself received as a reward for his fidelity. We can find in this action the summary and apex of a life totally turned to the Father and, consequently, totally turned to us.

If we try to isolate the basic components of prayer, we see that all Old Testament prayer fell into three broad categories. There was prayer of adoration and praise, prayer of thanksgiving and prayer of petition. To these the Eucharist adds yet a fourth category, that of atonement or reparation. These four aspects or movements of prayer should serve as guidelines as we approach God in prayer.

To speak of adoration and praise in the same breath is fitting, for they are practically synonymous. We show that we acknowledge and accept our creaturely relationship to God by extolling him, by rejoicing that he is God and Father. This praise is generally public. It is not a question only of interior movements of the mind but the ability to acknowledge God's rightful place in our lives in word and action. Jesus' entire life was one long hymn of praise to his Father. Throughout his life he attributed everything he did to him. His teaching was not his own, and he was able to say that he spoke only what the Father had revealed to him. At the beginning of his public life, Jesus proclaimed to the Samaritan woman that the hour was coming when all true worshipers would worship the Father in spirit and truth (Jn 4:23). That hour was the hour of his passion and death, an hour when Jesus himself was able to offer the ultimate act of adoration—his very life.

Closely akin to adoration is thanksgiving, which is a form of praise in gratitude for blessings received. This response to our being part of a covenant people in a world where God constantly reveals himself, is something that prevents us from taking life for granted. It enables us to see God as the source of all blessings and to maintain constant thanks for his action in our lives. In modern times, giving thanks tends to be only a verbal acknowledgment of debt, one discharged in private by mouth or letter. Children hear from their earliest years, "What do you say?" when some gift or service has been given. For the Hebrews, thanks was usually rendered publicly by telling everyone what marvelous things had been done. The good news was something shared.

The heart of the Eucharist is thanksgiving. Although the name itself is not found in the New Testament, the very word "eucharist" means thanksgiving. The implication is not only that Jesus' life was one of constant thanks to his Father for his goodness and protection, but that in and through Christ the Christian community's best way of thanking the Father is in recalling the blessings we have received by reason of Jesus' redemptive death/resurrection. From the beginning of the Eucharistic Prayer we acknowledge our duty to thank the Father through Jesus Christ his Son. We then begin to detail those various aspects of Jesus' life that we are focusing on at that particular celebration, and continue on to gratitude for having been counted worthy to stand in God's presence and serve him. We recall Jesus' own giving thanks over the bread and wine, knowing that this was his most characteristic attitude.

The ability which we have to make adoration and thanksgiving the cornerstone of our prayer life helps distinguish us from pagans. For among the many things that our religious tradition, especially the memorial of Christ's death, holds out to us is a legacy of wonder. The surest way to suppress our ability to understand the meaning of God and the importance of worship is to take things for granted. Indifference to the sublime wonder of living in God's grace is the root of sin.

A third great movement of prayer which characterizes the Eucharist (unlike Jewish prayer) is that of atonement. Jesus' death was redemptive and offered for our sins. The bread that is broken is Christ's body given up for us; the cup is the blood of the new covenant shed for us so that sin might be forgiven. St. Paul puts it succinctly: "Both Jew and pagan sinned and forfeited God's glory, and both are justified through the free gift of his grace by being redeemed in Christ Jesus who was appointed by God to sacrifice his life so as to win reconciliation through faith" (Rom 3:24-25).

It is not only the ability we have to acknowledge our sinfulness and to ask pardon for our failings that is considered a reparation. Reparation is the aspect of prayer that keeps us from being content with ourselves, which constantly impels us to serve God better. It is because of this that, despite repeated failure, we can continually recommit ourselves to the cause of Christ, and share *actively* in the Eucharist by striving each day to make our lives redemptive for others. We are called at each Mass to save the world, to share the bread which was broken.

Petition is the final movement of prayer. It comes only after the previous three. St. John's Gospel gives us the prayer of Jesus at the Last Supper (14-17). The

107

list of petitions here provides insights into the mind and heart of Christ, and why this prayer never fails; it is rooted in a total awareness of mission and acceptance of the Father's will. It is a search for that will. True prayer of petition, whether for self or for others, should always seek a change in ourselves or in our world, not in God. We are the ones who need to be opened up to a full appreciation of the Father's loving purpose. Petition enables us to truly pray, "Your will, not mine, be done."

The "eucharistic" prayer described here is not quiet, peaceful contemplation, although it should help provide a foundation for it. It flows from the Eucharist itself, and is made in its spirit. Doing this prevents our falling into pagan habits and attitudes, and links our private and public prayer. Even private prayer is something which should take us out of ourselves, enabling us to confront the realities of our Christian mission. In this Jesus gave the ultimate example. His most solemn prayer was uttered with nails in his hands and feet, surrounded by a hostile mob; to expect our prayer to be only a peaceful and relaxing experience of quiet closeness with God is to miss what it is all about.

XI

TAKING EUCHARIST HOME

We cannot live our life in church. And this should not bother us. The idea that the Eucharist is the source and summit of Christian life implies essentially two things.

First, it implies that it is the daily life that we live throughout the week that gives us something to bring to the community liturgy on Sundays. There we celebrate the reality of our incorporation in Christ; unless that incorporation is lived out consciously, there will be precious little to celebrate. We can't bring a worldly lifestyle, no different from that of our non-Christian friends and neighbors, to the altar and celebrate it as Christian.

The second aspect is that as *source*, the Eucharist should occupy a central part in every Christian life. It should influence the life that follows the celebration, so that gradually all one's values, ideals and daily life choices are derived from the Eucharist. In this way a rhythm is established. Inspired by the eucharistic celebration, the memory of Christ's action has a determinative influence on every aspect of our lives, so that we are qualitatively better prepared the following week to celebrate even greater dedication and to benefit more from sacramental contact with the Lord. This is made possible for us because our search for God is not one-sided. God does not stand by, silent and unconcerned. Not only has he adopted us as his children, but he has shared with us the very mission of his son Jesus. This awareness of our being called and depended on should make us eager to answer the challenge of God. The effort to live a consciously Christian life is made easier because of the fact that we are helped along the way by God himself. The memorial of Christ's death and resurrection which is the core of Eucharist assures us of that. The essence of a truly eucharistic life does not lie in entertaining our private ideas of union with God. It lies in the continuing ability to articulate a memory of moments of illumination by his presence. We are a people of witnesses of the glorious favor God has bestowed on us through his Son.

During the Eucharistic Prayer we always repeat Jesus' injunction to "do this in memory of me." This means far more than saying that we should all develop long historical memories (though that wouldn't hurt). In saying that the Eucharist is Christ's memorial, we are acknowledging that through his grace and power God is able even today to insert us into a past moment which is still living and actual. A past event is enabled to remain present and actual to subsequent generations.

Going beyond mental recall is made possible

because when God remembers, he acts. We are concerned here with active remembrance; God and man insert themselves in the accomplishments of the past. We must see to it that whatever is special and unique about the present is impregnated by what is equally unique in the past. We cannot stand at the foot of the cross with Mary. We are enabled to memorialize this, however, and know that God will repeat for his people today what he accomplished then. When God remembers, he displays his power. When we remember, we situate ourselves in the covenant action of Christ by responding to what God has done for us.

How can we respond? It is only possible by adapting daily concrete social behavior that is characterized by God's own behavior to us. We try to reflect this throughout each day. We communicate God's actions to others by doing for them what he continually does for us. Faithful obedience is active remembrance.

What this means is that the Eucharist and our daily lives do not belong to two separate categories or spheres. They are not only compatible with each other, they belong together. If life is not of whole cloth, both will suffer. The main themes of Eucharist and the main themes of life itself are one and the same. The Eucharist is not concerned with the realm of the holy and sacred while the main part of our lives is secular and profane. Jesus' Eucharist was not something he did only on the night before he died. It represented and reflected his entire life of self-giving. How could the church celebrate each day only a few hours of Jesus' life if this were not bound up with the rest? Eucharist is Jesus' memorial, the way of keeping alive and allowing us to share in his whole life. As for Jesus, so for us; if the Eucharist is only a one-hour-a-week ritual and not of one piece with the rest of our lives, we are liars, fools, or schizophrenics.

Living eucharistic lives is easy if we recall those four main movements of prayer which we mentioned in the last chapter. Our lives, all our prayers, words and actions, our ideals, hopes and dreams, can become part of a richly spiritual life if we strive to be people of *adoration, thanksgiving, reparation* and *petition.* This is not only the best possible way to live and pray, but it joins prayer and life into unity.

Because they are so closely related, let us consider adoration and thanksgiving together. Both are the foundation of any eucharistic life, rooting us in the consciousness that God is our Father, that we are his special people and that through Jesus we have been given rebirth. This is true faith. Faith comes from awe and wonder, from the awareness that we are exposed to God's loving presence. It arises out of a continuing anxiety to answer the challenge of God, out of an awareness that he continues to call us.

Our answer may have been given once, and perhaps renewed at Eucharist, but the commitment continues. Unless the awareness and memory of the ineffable mystery of our Christian existence becomes a permanent state of mind, our lives become faithless. The meaning of worship, of Eucharist, is its power to strengthen our alertness and refine our appreciation of the mystery.

This is especially important for us today. As civilization develops, a sense of wonder and thanks declines. Science has the answer to everything. But such a decline is an alarming symptom of our state of mind. Humankind will not perish for lack of facts or want of information, but only for want of appreciation. The beginning of our happiness lies in understanding that life without wonder and praise is not worth living. Our memorial of Jesus should reinforce in us the ability to discern how God is touching our lives. The constant struggle is to live not on the surface, but in active consciousness of our being in a godly universe. One of our goals should be to experience commonplace happenings and actions as part of our spiritual adventure, to feel God's hidden love and wisdom in all things.

In no way should this be taken as expounding an excessively simplistic way of blaming everything that happens in life on God. People who do this are to be congratulated on their God-centered lives, but they should be invited to greater realism in how he acts in our lives. Jesus once reminded us that God was a god of the living and not of the dead. We might carry that one step further and say that evil, sorrow and pain are the fruits of death, and in no way is God responsible for them. Our task here below is to increase the amount of life and grace, not adopt an unholy resignation to all that happens.

The motion of our minds and hearts to praise and glorify the Lord, to cultivate gratitude for his actions in our lives, is expressed at Mass; Eucharist itself then begins to be a real memorial, an active reliving of all the ways God has touched and continues to touch our human existence. Living in this way not only makes us more aware of the central place Jesus has in our lives, but it is the source of that joy and peace which only the Spirit of God can bring. It becomes a way of thinking, a frame of reference which unifies our life experience and allows us to integrate it into our Christian lives. All we do then becomes a means of expressing our total dependence on God and our gratitude for his ever-present love.

A word about personal prayer. Most people still pray today the way they did years ago. Now and then another prayer will be added to a long series of prayers that have been collected through the years. I sometimes think that we would do well to throw away all our prayers and keep only one: the Eucharist. For then we are reminded that God is the one who started the conversations; all he wants or expects is our response. Prayer should not be an elaborate or lengthy reliance on the words and sentiments of others. Is it not possible in the morning to take a few moments, to orient ourselves, to praise and thank God for a new day of living and loving, and to do this in our own words? We should never fear speaking to God in our own voice. He recognizes it and loves it. Prayer is the developed ability to tune in to God in our lives, and thank and praise him for his providence.

Closely linked to this is deepening our knowledge of God and bettering our response to him. Often known as spiritual reading, this was sometimes thought to be the private preserve of priests, religious and a few other chosen souls. Not so. It is necessary for all who want to base their lives on God. In trying to develop a spiritual reading program, it is good to remember that although many books are well written, our primary reading should be the Scriptures. God's word in the Eucharistic Prayer is powerful enough to cause Jesus to become present sacramentally. It is that same word proclaimed in the Scriptures that gives us an increased familiarity with how God has revealed himself. If the Sunday readings seem unfamiliar, however, and strangely irrelevant to our lives, it may be because we have done little to integrate them into our lives in any sustained way. We neither prepare or meditate on the weekly readings, nor do we deepen our understanding sufficiently of the living context from which they are taken. Were we more familiar with our forebears in faith, we would instinctively know how to serve God better in all we do.

This leads us to the third great movement of prayer: atonement and reparation. The church is built on the awareness of the expiatory power of Christ's death. We have truly been redeemed in his blood. We should be realistic here, however. In singing of Christ, "Being as all men are, he was humbler yet, even to accepting death, death on a cross" (Phil 2:8), we must be careful not to imagine God to be a bloodthirsty tyrant. Jesus accepted essentially two things: his human condition, and a life lived for others, and this involved suffering and death.

All human life grows out of situations we may not necessarily have chosen for ourselves, but that we accept and make our own as we mature. This leads to dominant choices. So also for Jesus. In accepting the consequences of his choices—to live for others— Jesus humbled himself and revealed the extent of his love by persevering in his choice even when it became obvious that it would result in his death. "A man can have no greater love than to lay down his life for his friends" (Jn 15:13). Suffering and sacrifice came into Jesus' life on the heels of his primary choice of an unselfish life.

When we celebrate the Eucharist, we immerse ourselves in this miracle of love and recognize it as a mystery of fidelity. Two sorts of daily events are involved here. The first set of events results from the basic choices we make in life: These dominant choices involve vocation, lifestyle, values and the commitment we should have for others. Most of our day-to-day life is a consequence of these choices. Another set of events that is often bound up with them is suffering and sorrow, the doubts, disappointment and discouragement that enter into daily life. The temptation for us, as it was for Jesus, is to change our basic orientation, to choose a different life and vocation, in order to avoid the pain. Fidelity to an unselfish life is not always easy.

Yet, it is important to integrate this aspect of our lives into Christ's own sacrifice. Prayer is the easiest way of doing this, for only reflection and conversation with God and with our ancestors in the faith enable us to make our lives purposeful and Christlike, not giving up when the day grows long. We have the assurance that a life lived for others is imitation of God himself. The memory of Christ's glorious resurrection and the Christian community born from his side are the primary examples of how even suffering can be redemptive.

The notion of atonement, however, is also one that facilitates many of our moral choices. When faced with alternative and sometimes difficult choices, we often retreat (if possible) to the law or the commandments. It would be easier if we saw all choices as proceeding from our most basic choice for Jesus and for others. Anything which strengthens that basic orientation is good, while anything which weakens our dominant choice is bad and should be avoided. This helps give meaning and purpose even to areas of life that seemed far removed from "church." It also helps integrate our lives so that worship and life are like the ebb and flow of the same tide.

The final element in a truly eucharistic life is the area of petition. Life is the central message of the Eucharist, and this true Christian life is our main concern. As mentioned in the last chapter, we should avoid petitioning like pagans, praying in any way that tries to manipulate God. Eucharistic petition helps us to avoid this, especially because it flows from a deep sense of adoration and thanksgiving as well as atonement. Our habitual concerns and petitions reveal to what extent we are fully eucharistic in mind and heart.

Jesus' prayer of petition, even in the hour of his greatest pain, was almost entirely turned to others. He prayed that his disciples' faith might not fail, and that they might accept hatred and opposition; he forgave his executioners and prayed that we might all be one. It was a confident prayer, rooted in his mission as servant. We need to learn to imitate not only the content of Jesus' prayer, but its reality as well. Jesus did not pray off in some corner and expect the answer to come from heaven like the rain. He invested himself in his prayer; he became part of what he prayed for. St. James captured this insight in more homely terms when he told us that if we see a brother or sister who has nothing to wear and no food for the day and all our prayer consists in is: "I wish you well; keep yourself warm and eat plenty," while doing nothing to meet the person's bodily needs, what good is it? (Jas 2:14-17).

It is the same for us who are aware of the needs of our world. It is easy to pray for peace in the world or for starving people in the Third World. But if this prayer is made in the isolation of our own air-conditioned splendor and we do nothing concrete to change the situation, our prayer is thoroughly lifeless. Eucharist shows us that Jesus was very much a part of his prayer. It also shows that concern for others is part of a wholly integrated life, a eucharistic life.

Other traditional works of piety are important, and perhaps more should have been said of them. They are all, however, only *means*, never ends in themselves. We should use those necessary to truly live our Eucharist, knowing a truly eucharistic life is one that joins us with Jesus in his final hour, with arms outstretched as if to embrace the world he lived and died for, knowing that we have our own part to play in that mission. Accepting this is what keeps the Eucharist alive and makes it the source and summit of truly Christian life.

XII

LIVING A EUCHARISTIC LIFE

St. Cyril of Alexandria once said, "Fundamentally the Eucharist is a victory—a victory of one who is absent to become present in a world which conceals him." The Eucharist is the sacramental way Jesus has found to transcend time and space. In the days of his earthly life, Jesus was present in the flesh. His physical presence was a historically verifiable reality, and during his public ministry he went about doing good in this or that locality. All that came to an end when his human existence was snuffed out on Calvary. It is the Eucharist that guarantees that his presence among us will not cease. Yet, the ability of Jesus to be victorious through the ages is not automatic. It depends to a large extent on whether we allow him the victory for which he died and rose.

All of us at one time or another have thought of the Eucharist and wondered how Jesus could possibly be present in a piece of bread or a cup of wine. Despite

119

everything which we have been taught about the real presence of Jesus, the inability of proving or even imagining how this can be is troubling at times. Doubts and fears arise. And the seeming downplaying of Christ's eucharistic presence in the days that followed Vatican II is not reassuring. What can we do to deepen our understanding of and appreciation for the wonder of Christ's presence?

It is important to remember that there is nothing magical about the Eucharist. We should carefully avoid thinking of Jesus as being up in heaven at the beck and call of every priest who offers Mass. During and because of the Eucharistic Prayer, Jesus does not suddenly become present where he did not exist before; he does not appear in a vacuum; he does not leap from heaven to earth. Rather, his eucharistic presence is situated within a whole network of relationships, a matrix of interconnected presences in and for the community. Depending on the depth and reality of our own Christ-life, we actually condition the possibility and reality of Christ's presence in our world. We can impede or hasten his victory.

The Vatican Council as well as Pope Paul VI's encyclical on the Eucharist have confused the issue for some by introducing new terminology. In their effort to clarify the nature of Jesus' eucharistic presence, they reminded us that there are many other "real" presences of Christ in the world. In other words, there are different ways in which Jesus is present to us, and all of these are related to the Eucharist, where these modes of presence all converge and where they are transcended by Jesus' sacramental action and presence.

Speaking of other ways in which Christ is "really" present should not make us think that the eucharistic presence is less real in any way. The church itself simply wants us to appreciate more and more the wealth and beauty of what we might call the *total* mystery of Jesus' lordship over his church. We are doing the mystery an injustice if we compartmentalize it or reduce it to any one component element, such as Mass, Communion, or Real Presence. To limit our understanding of Jesus' presence in the Eucharist to a form of local presence is also too restricting and static. The eucharistic presence goes beyond saying that Jesus is "there" in that host or tabernacle, to realizing that we are speaking of contact with the living Lord himself, body and blood. This is a personal encounter with the risen Christ, and as such requires our own presence and response as well.

The Eucharist is Jesus' gift to his brothers and sisters, to the members of his own body, the church. This gift is offered to those in whom he already dwells by his Spirit. It is the summit of all the other modes of presence. It is given to nourish life already begun. Consequently, there is a reciprocity which takes place. The various other modes of presence all come together in the Eucharist. They flourish there because they are nourished by it and because they make sense only when vivified by the rich interpersonal encounter with the risen Lord that only Eucharist makes possible.

Although the documents of the church may list many ways in which Jesus continues to serve his Mystical Body, let us isolate three which are more closely related to the actual celebration of the Eucharist. In this way we can see how they are related, how they enrich each other and how our own lives can become more eucharistic in the fullest sense of the word.

In speaking of Jesus' presence, we cannot stress sufficiently that it is an *offered* presence. It is offered to those gathered to celebrate the mystery of their being church. A sacrament of spiritual communion and communication, it is far more important than mere physical proximity. The sacramental closeness and actual reception of Communion in the course of the liturgy is not an end in itself; it is to nourish the inner life of those who receive. To link Jesus' presence with the faithful gathered to increase the depth of their union with him in this way is to stress the importance and necessity of a believing community. Jesus is already present in those gathered in his name. The faith of the assembly, and its desire to truly *be* the Body of Christ, is a major aspect of Eucharist.

This presence of Christ in the community is the concrete result of baptism. St. Augustine captured this reality graphically many years ago. In his 272nd sermon, he said, "If you are the Body of Christ and his members, it is your mystery which has been placed on the altar of the Lord; you receive your own mystery. You answer 'Amen' to what you are." The members of Christ's body are not only joined to one another, their very life comes from the breath of the Spirit of Jesus. There is a mutual relationship between this body and the Eucharist, which is both the sign of oneness in the Lord as well as the context wherein that unity is actualized and deepened.

The quote from St. Augustine serves to remind us that there is a "more and less" aspect of our being part of the Body of Christ. We know that the struggle to "put on Christ," as St. Paul says, is a lifelong one; it is never-ending. Precisely here does the eucharistic presence of Christ urge us on, challenging us to respond more fully to the mystery which is ours. If our faith is weak, and the quality of our lives barely Christ-like, Jesus' presence within will not be very obvious. On the other hand, as we grow into the likeness of Christ and bring to the Eucharist a faith-filled presence, the eucharistic Christ will more and more become enfleshed within us. We will be saying "Amen" to a reality which is visible for all to see; we will become more fully one in Christ.

If Christ's community presence is essential for an integral eucharistic celebration, another mode of presence which enters in is Jesus' presence in the person of the priest who presides over the assembly. This is an interesting mode of presence because it forces us to ask what it means to minister at the altar. In an ecumenical age, what seems to concern people most about this question is whether or not the priest is validly ordained. Does he have the power to bring about transubstantiation? While not denying either the importance or necessity of ordination in the community of the church, we cannot be satisfied with a theology of power ("Who has the power to do what to whom?"). Thinking in terms of power or validity can result in a theology and spirituality of words and gestures quite apart from their living context as expressions of the church.

If Christ is actually present in the priest at the altar, it means that, as the officially commissioned representative of the universal brotherhood of faith which is the church, the priest is the visible sign of both the believing community and the head of that community, Christ himself. He is especially an active sign of Jesus who continues to gather his own together to share in his banquet.

Catholic theology has traditionally said that the priest acts *in persona Christi*, in the person of Christ. This is a many-faceted statement. For the priest stands at the altar not only as representative of the community, but as the living sign of Christ making it possible for two or three to gather in his name. This ability to preside flows from the rest of a life which should also parallel that of Jesus. Because of his work in the parish or community, the priest is the ordinary means of sharing Christ's mercy and compassion. Already exercising a presidency of charity among the people, as did Jesus, when he moves from the concerns of everyday parish life to the liturgical articulation of this same community's public prayer, he does so as one who mirrors Christ's own continuing service of the brethren.

All of this is part of the experience of church. The priest does not act as a soloist, apart and easily separable from the community for which he was ordained. His power is the ability to articulate the actuality of the community's life and also the relationship of Christ to that same community. At the altar he ritually celebrates all the relationships which bind Christ to his body and the members to each other and to Christ himself. He never acts as an isolated individual.

Thus, Christ's eucharistic presence cannot be separated from these two other modes of presence. For it is Christ's body, the church, which his eucharistic presence is intended to nourish, and in which he is already present by faith and love, as well as the action of the Holy Spirit. Also, the priest is the one who presides over and unifies the community; Jesus uses him to gather his own in his arms and continue his saving work throughout history. When both priest and community gather, however, we are aware of yet a third major way in which Jesus strives to accomplish his victory over the world: Christ is also present in the word of God which is proclaimed.

In the liturgy, pride of place is given to the word of God in Scripture and in the Eucharistic Prayer. For this reason the Vatican insists that all non-scriptural compositions be used only to coordinate, reinforce or interpret the thoughts of the scriptural passages. This is because the liturgy uses Scripture in the light of Christ, that is, it sees Jesus as the fulfillment and culmination of salvation history and as the key to understanding all of revelation.

After the Scriptures are proclaimed, we are invited to praise God because we have just shared his word. Scripture is likewise a record of the human response given through the ages to God's self-revelation. It is the word of God inasmuch as it reveals the human answer in faith to this word. Our answer takes up God's word and gives testimony to it by giving it living expression. It is a vital testimony to the power and presence of the Holy Spirit guiding our search.

Christ's presence in the word, however, is not brought to a close when the priest has concluded the homily. The supreme realization of God's saving word is yet to take place in the radical commitment of the church to God which we call the Eucharistic Prayer. Together with the proclamation of the word in Scripture this is the final interlocking phase of our celebration of salvation.

Our eucharistic encounter with Christ is made possible only in the Eucharistic Prayer, that "thanksgiving" which is a word pronounced in Christ as well as a word pronounced by his ecclesial body. The Lord himself acts in this word through the power of the Holy Spirit. It is during and because of the Eucharistic Prayer that Christ's sacramental presence is effected. This interpenetration of the efficacy of the word and of the Holy Spirit during Mass encompasses our entire life of faith. We strive to be faithful to God's law of love because we have been moved by his word. Thanks to the Holy Spirit, the efficacy of that word is geared to our daily life, to our truly living the Christ-life more fully each living moment.

This is why we can call the Eucharist the sacrament of faith, not because we need much faith in order to believe it, but because everything meant by and evoked by faith is expressed by it. It should also be obvious that the eucharistic presence of Christ is not his sudden appearance in a place where he was heretofore absent. He was already present in the assembly, in the priest and in his word. His presence is intensified and given the ability to become the saving reality of the body and blood that was offered on the cross for our salvation.

Why does Jesus give himself to us in such a complete and total fashion? In order to evoke a corresponding totality in each of us. He wants us to make him present in a world which would otherwise conceal him.

This highlights an important consideration, one

that is often neglected. In thinking of Christ's real eucharistic presence, we cannot but be aware that he is not actually among us the way people are usually present to each other. The historical Christ is really absent; yet, he has been able to use the sacramental world to conquer the distance that separates his risen state from that of his body on earth. His sacramental presence is a form of interpersonal presence, that of one person to another. It necessarily requires a response of the faithful because it is intended to make them instruments of salvation to their full capacity.

In this sense, Jesus' presence is offered to us and awaits a response from us, an acceptance, a recognition of love and faith. Without that it is like a hand offered in friendship that is never clasped. Unless the assembly and each of us recognize Jesus in his sacrament and appreciate the purpose of his continued presence in our world, there is no real encounter that takes place between us and the Lord. This encounter that Jesus seeks to bring about is the heart of the eucharistic mystery.

Anything short of person-to-person encounter reduces Christ's presence to a form of local presence. It is no different from being elbow to elbow with a stranger in a subway. One might as well be standing next to a packing crate. Jesus awaits our recognition and our response. This response is not demonstrated by warm feelings or external manifestations of piety and reverence. It is shown, rather, by a free and total acceptance of the law of the new covenant. It says that our faith is living and active enough for us to live as Jesus lived and to love one another as he has loved us.

The communion that takes place between us and Jesus in the heart of this encounter is the Christian celebration of covenant.

These realities deserve reflection from time to time. A truly eucharistic life, one centered on Jesus, can never be satisfied with only a partial view of the mystery of faith. Understanding and highlighting other ways in which Christ is really present to us is important because all of these are part of the total lordship of Jesus over his church.

Furthermore, neglecting the varied modes of Christ's presence can cause us to stress one at the expense of the others. When we honor all the ways in which Jesus continues to direct his people, however, we find that our understanding of each of them grows and deepens, enabling a fuller response to the sacrament itself. We must guard, for example, against exercising total reverence and dedication to Christ present in the Eucharist while failing to honor his presence in our sisters and brothers in whom he also dwells. The eucharistic presence is not some object or person that we keep and worship; it is part of the total reality of Christ's presence to his people—a far richer concept.

Another benefit is that this awareness reminds us of the *purpose* of Christ's presence. The actual, interpersonal contact that Jesus hopes to elicit and sustain is something we must cooperate with. Our own personal participation in the mystery is essential. We are brought face to face with Christ as were the first Christians or any of those who heard and saw him when he walked the streets of Palestine. Our responses can be as varied as theirs. We can ignore him, pick and choose the things that we like, or commit ourselves entirely to him in loving response. It is this total response that Jesus seeks and wants. Otherwise, the sacramental perpetuation of his saving life will have been a glorious idea without fulfillment.

In final analysis, when we ask how Jesus is going to conquer the distance that separates his glorious state from our own, and how the Eucharist can be a victory of one who is absent to become present in a world which conceals him, we know that we are the ones who can facilitate or delay the final victory. The eucharistic presence of Christ is at the heart of the church. But it will be a redeeming presence for us only if the whole mystery of Christ's life is accepted and lived. Only in this way will the church become the presence of Christ in the world.

XIII

BREAD FOR A NEW WORLD

The existing world order (or disorder) is contrary to the values of the Eucharist. Poverty, hunger and suffering are unfortunate facts of life for most of the world's population. The world system is greedily exploitative, whereas the Eucharist implies loving sharing. World relations destroy persons and peoples, whereas the Eucharist builds community. The world is racist, whereas the Eucharist is universalist. The international scene is marked by arrogant domination, where the Eucharist is the sacrament of humble service.

The eucharistic bread is intended for the multitudes; in the world bread is just another commodity for trade. Is it possible to continue celebrating Eucharist and remain unconcerned about national and international poverty and injustice? Is this what Jesus wanted?

Eucharist asks too little of people today. It is ready to offer comfort; it has little courage to challenge. It is ready to console and edify; it has little ability to break complacency, to shatter our callousness.

Perhaps the trouble is that the Eucharist has become "religion"—institution, dogma, security. It is not an *event* anymore. Its celebration involves neither risk nor strain. It has become orthodox; respectability has been achieved. It is not a drama anymore; it is routine. Uniqueness is suppressed and repetitiveness prevails. Unless we renew our sense of the Eucharist's significance, the ultimate preciousness of our own existence disappears. Christian life becomes meaningless.

One of the central problems of the age is emptiness of heart, a decreased sensitivity to the call of the Spirit, the collapse of challenge between the realm of tradition and the inner world of the individual. We do not know how to think, how to pray, how to cry, or how to resist the deception of living in conformity to the values and lifestyle of the world around us. Eucharist should counteract this trivialization of existence. Involving, as it does, our relationship with Jesus and with each other, it should give us a sense of living in ultimate relationships. It should teach us how to stand alone and not be alone; it should reveal God as a refuge and strength, not a security blanket.

Eucharist stands out against the deflation of mankind. Jesus shows us that we are capable of sacrifice, discipline, of moral and spiritual courage. We are capable of ultimate commitment. This ultimate commitment includes the consciousness that we are accountable for all our actions, for whether or not they create a better world. We must be aware that what we own we owe. We need a capacity for conversion and repentance. We should be convinced that life without the service of God and neighbor is a scandal. Yes, the Eucharist cries out against the trivialization of existence. Who will hear its cry?

Some are prevented from hearing its cry because they still relegate the Eucharist to church and sanctuary, a sacred refuge within a profane world. The Eucharist joins us to Jesus and his Passover sacrifice; it is a source of grace, our personal worship of the Father. What has it to do with the world outside? Hence resistance—and resentment—often follows any mention from the pulpit of politics, or race relations, or social justice. In fact, churches stressing social outreach have barely held their own in the past 20 years. Churches that had a narrow view of the sacred, on the other hand, that promised salvation in return for fidelity, that had no ecumenical or social outreach, all increased in membership in the '60s and '70s.

Others who do not hear the cry are those for whom religion is essentially a personal relationship with God, and who are uncomfortable with the more recent communitarian stress since the Vatican Council. The time of Mass is time alone with God. Salvation tends to focus more on avoiding the wrong (sin) than in doing the right.

Those who do hear are those who take seriously two of Jesus' requests associated with the Eucharist: one, that we repeat his self-sacrificing love as his memorial; the second, that we become distributors of the bread he has provided. Both statements are aspects of Christian mission and are correlative to each other. In the period of the church the blessings of salvation and liberation are distributed by the disciples, or people will die for want of them.

Our attitudes may prevent Jesus' ability to heal and nourish life, however, from being extended as it could. The fact that this was a problem in the early church as well as now is obvious from St. Mark's Gospel. Human nature must constantly be challenged by Jesus' own values and Mark's Gospel helps us to do that. Most commentators call the section in his Gospel from chapter 6:31 through 8:26 the "bread section," because it is framed by the two stories of Jesus providing food for the multitudes. In both cases, there is plenty left over. In Mark's first account there are 12 full baskets.

Some questions Mark would like us to ask are: Why is there so much left over? What will happen to it? Who is responsible for seeing that it is used as Jesus intended? The last question is the easiest to answer. The fact that 12 baskets remained of Christ's bread neatly provides one for each apostle. It is the task of the apostles down through the ages to distribute the blessings which Jesus came to bring. This they are to do generously, to all in need, as Jesus himself had done. On many occasions Jesus had demonstrated the extent to which he reached out to all. The scandal which he provoked by eating with the lower classes or the oppressed is already well known. Jesus did not feel the need to defend his own practice; he insisted others should imitate him. One middle-class host was told he ought to invite to his table "the poor, the crippled, the lame, the blind" rather than friends, relatives or wealthy neighbors (Lk 14:12-14). Jesus surely preached what he himself practiced.

Mark answers the question of why so much is left over by pointing out a breakdown in distribution and explains why this is so. The first reason is developed at the beginning of chapter 7. There we are told that the ritualism that religion can lead to is one of the root causes of the breakdown. The pharisaic school had developed such a series of rules and interpretations regarding meals that the world of legal impurities effectively excluded many who were hungry. Jesus calls this hypocritical because human traditions have become substituted for God's real intentions. The worst thing about this type of exclusion is that it is done with a clear conscience. In fact there is more than a degree of self-righteousness involved, as people who dare to do otherwise are criticized and looked down on.

The transposition to our own day is obvious, and it is a danger that must be guarded against because it is so easy to fall into, mistaking it for reverence or for the will of God. The attitude reveals itself in both the liturgical and social areas. Liturgically, it is far easier to concentrate on externals, on rubrics, on the exact composition of the bread or other such details than it is on the ultimate reality being celebrated. It is also easier by far to catalogue those who are worthy to receive Communion. There must be some form of monumental arrogance involved in thinking in terms of worthiness of sharing Christ's cup and salvation!

Tied in with the liturgical area, however, is the social. How many people never enter into our world simply because they are outside the "legal limits" we have set for Christian concern? We narrowly define for ourselves what is required for salvation, and this does not usually include the neighbor—especially the distant neighbor. Our view of Christian responsibility is narrowly circumscribed, and so is our world view. At the same time, like the Pharisees, we piously go about our daily lives in the comfortable assumption that we are pleasing to God. In this section of Mark's Gospel, he berates those who neglect to support their parents on religious pretext (7:9-13). Our own examples today are just as glaring.

As to why we develop this narrowness, Jesus provides a clue. After shocking everyone by saying that nothing external can render anyone impure (remember the violent conflicts this caused in the early church in regard to kosher dietary laws), he went on to say that sin alone renders anyone impure because it springs from the recesses of the heart. It also prevents us from appreciating the plight of others, for among these sins are greed, maliciousness, deceit, envy, arrogance and an obtuse spirit (7:14-23).

Even if we succeeded in rooting out the preceding disorders, however, there would still be bread left over. Mark gives us a second reason when he brings in the Syro-Phoenician woman at this point (7:24-30). She was a pagan, but was still able to share in the crumbs, the leftovers from the table prepared for Jesus' people. It took years for the implication of this to register. Perhaps it still hasn't fully taken root. But the danger is an obvious one: restricting salvation—food—only to "the chosen people." Our horizons are limited to our own parish, or church, or religious group rather than to all in need without limit. Eucharist should enable us to reach out to the needy, wherever they might be.

There is a mean and petty streak in all of us. The miracles of the loaves and of the Eucharist tell us of the abundance with which Jesus graces us, abundance that is such that there is more than enough for everyone. There is always the fear, however, that we will be depriving ourselves. One of the Old Testament passages which Mark surely had in mind when telling the story of the loaves articulates the same fear. In 2 Kings 4:42-44, the prophet Elisha tells his servant to set bread before 100 hungry men. He was met with the protest that there wasn't enough to go around—just as the disciples wanted Jesus to dismiss the crowd for the same reason. But, "Thus says the Lord," Elisha insisted, "they shall eat and there shall be some left over!" That is still true today.

Isolationism and a fend-for-yourself philosophy have no place in Christian behavior, especially if they are motivated by lack of faith in the gift of God. We should never fear giving even the little that we have, because there will always be some left over. The ability to share, knowing that all we have is gift, is the mark of a true disciple. The willingness to include others in the blessings we have received is what keeps those same benefits fruitful for us as well.

To say we believe in Jesus today is to live his Eucharist the way he would have us live it. Unless Jesus and what he stands for occupy first place in our value system, we have denied him and everything he lived and died for. To say that Jesus is divine, and that the Eucharist is the sacramentally actual presence of that same Lord, is to proclaim externally that he is the one we base our lives on. If our lives give lie to this affirmation, we are deceivers.

On the Feast of Corpus Christi, St. Thomas Aquinas shares a few thoughts with us on the significance of the Eucharist. "The only Son of God," he wrote, "wanted to have us share his divinity, and therefore he took our nature to himself.... Furthermore, what he took of our nature he gave back to us for our salvation." How can we share in Christ's divinity? By living his life given in baptism, by imitating his behavior, by adopting his values, by basing our lives on what he lived for.

We must throw out all our preconceived ideas of what God is all about, of what holiness is all about, of what is sacred. The only way we really have of knowing what it means to be divine is to look at Jesus. We deceive ourselves if we imagine what Jesus is like from what we think God is supposed to be like. In reality, to believe that Jesus is divine is not to change anything we know about Jesus from the Scriptures; it is to change our understanding of divinity itself and of what it means to be holy. By looking at Christ, we can begin to realize that our images of the sacred are perhaps not what God is at all. And our views of holiness and worship are just as much in need of correction.

Jesus did not live in two worlds, one sacred and one profane. He did not lead two lives, one holy and one secular. The Incarnation destroyed that distinction. The only things in life which are incompatible with a true following of Christ are those preconceived ideas we have of what importance, rank and leadership are all about. The disciples had a terribly difficult time appreciating what Jesus' messiahship was all about. Each time he spoke of his coming sufferings, Mark shows them completely misunderstanding what was going on.

After the first prediction, the main problems are

unwillingness to sacrifice or suffer for others. But Jesus cautions against excessive concern for self-preservation and the accumulation of wealth (Mk 8:35-36). The second prediction shows that misunderstanding of what it means to be a follower of Jesus comes also from jealousy and chauvinism, as well as a desire to enhance one's own importance (9:35-38). The final prediction falls on deaf ears because the disciples' main concerns at the time are the petty rivalries within the community, a desire for personal glory and the top leadership positions.

Jesus tried to show them that this was not what discipleship was all about by pointing to the example of his own life. The lesson should not be lost on us. He did not want to be given status and rank in our world; instead he took the lowest place, that of one who serves. He did not want honor and acclaim; he asked to be recognized in the poor and weak, with whom he has chosen to identify himself in a spirit of love and compassion.

The Eucharist has an extraordinary potential for bringing about personal and global transformation. If ever it is vitalized into being a sacrament of communion through effective personal sharing, it can successfully challenge the comfortable cultural values most people blindly accept. If Christians ever begin to practice what Jesus has taught and exemplified when he took, blessed, broke and gave bread to be distributed, many of the world's problems would be solved at both personal and institutional levels.

A true Eucharist is never a passive, comforting moment alone with God, something which allows us to escape the cares and concerns of our everyday life.

Eucharist is where all these cares and concerns come to a focus, and where we are asked to measure them against the standard lived by Jesus when he proclaimed for all to hear that the bread that he would give would provide life for the entire world. But it will do so only if, finding ourselves with a basket of bread, we have peered deeply enough into the heart of Christ to know what to do with it.